Charlie White's 103 Fishing Secrets

Charlie White's 103 Fishing Secrets

Illustrations by Nelson Dewey

Heritage
House

National Library of Canada Cataloguing in Publication Data

White, Charles, 1925-
Charlie White's 103 fishing secrets / Charlie White.

ISBN 1-895811-61-9

1. Fishing. 2. Fishing—British Columbia. I. Title. II. Title:
103 fishing secrets. III. Title: One hundred and three fishing
secrets.
SH441.W56 2003   799.1   C 98-910137-1

First edition 1985, second edition 2003.

Heritage House acknowledges the financial support for our
publishing program from the Government of Canada through
the Book Publishing Industry Development Program (BPIDP),
Canada Council for the Arts, and the British Columbia Arts
Council.

Cover design: Darlene Nickull
Cover photos: Front, Peter Sara; back, Marianne Scott
Illustrations: Nelson Dewey
Layout design: Katherine Hale

HERITAGE HOUSE PUBLISHING COMPANY LTD.
Unit #108 - 17665 66A Ave., Surrey, BC, V3S 2A7

Printed in Canada

BRITISH
COLUMBIA
ARTS COUNCIL
We acknowledge the support of the Province of British Columbia
through the British Columbia Arts Council

The Canada Council | Le Conseil des Arts
for the Arts | du Canada

CONTENTS

DEDICATION 6

ACKNOWLEDGEMENTS 6

INTRODUCTION 7

Chapter One
GENERAL CONSIDERATIONS 15

Chapter Two
PREPARING FOR A FISHING TRIP 25

Chapter Three
FINDING THE FISH 39

Chapter Four
BETWEEN YOU AND THE BOTTOM 53

Chapter Five
TROLLING TECHNIQUES 73

Chapter Six
FISHING WITH BAIT 97

Chapter Seven
MATURE SALMON IN RIVER-MOUTH AREAS . . . 103

Chapter Eight
STRIKING, PLAYING, AND LANDING A FISH . . . 111

Chapter Nine
CONCLUSIONS 129

Chapter Ten
FUTURE PLANS 137

OBTAINING CURRENT FISHING REGULATIONS . . . 139

CHARLIE WHITE'S FISHING LOG 140

DEDICATION

I dedicate this book to my mother, who has supported and encouraged my interest in fishing and wildlife since my "fishing fever" began when I was five years old. She tolerated my 3 a.m. departures for the local pond, the messy basement washtubs in which I cleaned the catch, and even the hooks and worms left in my pockets.

ACKNOWLEDGEMENTS

Everyone who taught me something about fishing—and that includes *all* my fishing partners—deserves my thanks, because I learn something on every fishing trip. Special thanks to Rhys Davis, Charlie Guiguet, and Lee and Patty Hallberg, who showed me the basics of salmon fishing.

Thanks also to those who helped develop the underwater TV system that revealed so much about salmon behaviour: Allan Hook, Roger and Tony Rose, Nick Dominique, Laraine Frances, Mike Shack, Bruce Colegrave, Jack Lugg, my sons Chad, Kevin, and David, and the gang at Sony.

I also acknowledge those who did so much in preparation of this book—Nelson Dewey, Sally Constable, Tim Cyr, Rex Armstead, Mary S. Aikins, and the staff at Special Interest Publications.

Special thanks to my beautiful and dedicated wife, Darlene, who supports me in everything I do. She (and my son David) nursed me back to health after a devastating stroke left me partially paralyzed in 1999.

—Charlie White

INTRODUCTION

Webster's Dictionary has many definitions of the word "secret," the most prominent being "kept from knowledge or view," "something kept hidden or unexplained." Another— "revealed only to the initiated"—is more appropriate in this instance, as much of the information in this book is already known to experienced and so-called expert anglers.

This book is a compilation of the tips and "secrets" I learned from experts when I first started fishing; the knowledge I have acquired from my own fishing experiences; and, especially, the things I have learned and continue to learn from my research with an underwater television camera.

Boyhood experiences

I have been fishing for more than 70 years, having started with a bobber and worm in the ponds and streams of Pennsylvania and Ohio when I was six years old. For the next twenty years I fished enthusiastically for carp, catfish, sunfish, blue gills, creek suckers, chubs, rock bass, walleye, pike, and perch. I even had the occasional battle with smallmouth and largemouth bass.

On several occasions I travelled to Ontario for some exciting fishing for larger bass, great northern pike, and deep-running lake trout. During a stint with the U. S. Navy, I fished for cod off Nova Scotia.

Life-cycle studies

In those days, fishing was the most intense of a number of personal hobbies, but it became the core of my life after I moved to the west coast in 1948. I became obsessed with salmon fishing, ultimately spending two years with the Oregon Fish Commission as a biologist-photographer. I fin-clipped young salmon in hatcheries and then followed them through their entire life cycles. I learned a great deal from the other biologists, who were also keen anglers in their spare time.

After moving to Vancouver Island, British Columbia, in 1956, fishing became even more important to me. I had moved to Victoria primarily to build and operate a television station, but there is no doubt that my move was strongly influenced by the good fishing nearby.

Fishing guide

When the station was completed, I moved full-time into fishing projects. I operated a fishing charter business during the summer and designed marine products (crab traps, sinkers, and bait boxes) during the off-season.

Being a guide was not the easygoing occupation I thought it would be. In fact, it can entail more pressure than that experienced by most business executives. Yet I quickly established a reputation for consistent success using light tackle (much sport fishing in those days was done with heavy wire lines and cannon balls) and attracted many "executive parties" from such places as Victoria's Empress Hotel and through the tourist bureau.

Some groups would fly in by private jet, rush by taxi to the marina, and we would be off to the fishing grounds. If we didn't have a fish in the boat within the first 30 minutes, some of the high-powered execs would begin tapping their feet on the deck and drumming their fingers on the arms of their seats. Not a word was spoken (usually), but I knew they were thinking, "Well, Mr. Expert, where's the fish?" Mercifully, the fishing was usually pretty good, and I had developed some quite successful strategies, which I will explain later in the book. There were, however, too many occasions when the fishing was really tough, and my tension level soared as I scrambled to get that first fish on board.

There are no relaxing days on the water. The customer doesn't really care about the big catch you made last week, or the exciting run of giant salmon due at the end of the month. He wants fish in the box today!

All of this activity was a far cry from my formal education: I had obtained a degree in civil engineering from Cornell University in New York state, and then practised engineering for two years prior to moving to the west coast. This training gave me the necessary background to develop an exciting new project. This project was conceived while talking with charter guests who regularly expressed great curiosity not only about salmon, but about all marine life and the underwater environment.

Undersea observations

The project was the development of the Pacific Undersea Gardens in Victoria, a unique marine exhibit something like an aquarium in reverse. Essentially, it is a large steel chamber into which the public descends to watch marine life in a more natural environment. A fence around the chamber keeps marine creatures close enough for viewing.

After building the first Undersea Gardens (three more were eventually constructed, one each in Washington, Oregon, and California), I spent hundreds of hours watching salmon and other marine creatures. I learned about their feeding habits in relation to tidal action, time of day, and availability of food. I was not, however, completely satisfied with these observations, and I continued to look for a way to observe salmon behaviour, underwater, in the wild.

Then one day while shopping at a local drugstore, I noticed a small surveillance camera used to detect shoplifters. Suddenly I was struck with the idea of using such a camera underwater. I was developing the Scotty downrigger at the time and thought that I could hook this tiny camera on the downrigger wire and watch my lures in action. We designed and constructed a special housing and lowered the apparatus under my boat. The first unit leaked, and a mass of foam boiled out of the housing when we opened it. Salt water, electric current, and delicate circuit boards just don't mix.

The next housing worked well enough, but we got only pictures of the bottom of the boat and propellers. Finally we got the camera working, then spent months overcoming control problems so we could keep it aimed at the trolling lure.

I'll never forget the first time everything worked properly. I was sitting in the cockpit of the boat, watching a television monitor as my lure moved through the water almost 40 feet below. My dream was actually coming true. I could watch what every fisherman has dreamed of: the actual moment of strike.

As we watched the screen, a fish suddenly loomed behind the lure. At first we couldn't figure out what kind of fish it was, but then we realized it was a salmon. But the salmon was swimming *upside down,* approaching the lure on its back. We were so excited that the helmsman left the wheel and the boat began weaving in slow circles around the bay.

The fish approached the lure several times, then veered off. We thought we had already made a dramatic discovery about salmon behaviour: They apparently rolled over onto their backs to strike a lure. This seemed possible when I remembered films about sharks in the South Pacific, footage that showed them rolling over on their backs to attack the belly of a fleeing baitfish.

We quickly hauled the gear to the surface so we could rush off and announce our exciting discovery to the whole fishing world. But when we got the gear to the surface, we discovered that the cables had tangled, and it was the *camera* that was upside down.

After a lot more trial and error, we got the system operating reasonably well and began to learn some things that fishermen have wondered about for thousands of years. For the first time, we were able to watch, close up and in slow motion, fish approach and strike (or turn away from) our lures.

Almost immediately we debunked one of the most prevalent theories of most fishing experts. Popular wisdom had it that a salmon always grabs a bait or lure by the head (to kill it, they said), as tooth marks are often found near the front end of lures. However, our camera showed salmon consistently grabbing all lures from the tail. Even those that approached the lure from the side would usually circle around from behind and attack directly from the rear. This had all kinds of implications for lure design and hook placement.

We also disproved the theory that salmon slap the bait with their tails before striking. We often saw salmon rush a lure, then turn away at the last minute with their tails whipping past it. However, on closer scrutiny of these shots in slow motion, we found that the fish never touched the lure. Apparently, they were just giving it a close inspection and turning away at the last possible moment.

In analyzing these same shots we discovered that the fish always passed with its lateral line in close proximity to the moving lure. Biologists speculate that they are somehow sensing the vibration or density of the lure with their lateral line as they pass close to it. We hope to investigate this phenomenon more thoroughly to help us in future lure design.

We also made some discoveries about the importance of sharp hooks, proper fishing depth, and lure action; we will cover these in the main body of this book.

Chapter One
GENERAL CONSIDERATIONS

Several years ago, a most unusual book became a bestseller. Titled *Inner Tennis,* it dealt with the importance of attitude and confidence in improving your game. There is no doubt that a positive attitude is also extremely important to fishing success. If you expect success, you are much more likely to have it. This is true in tennis, fishing, or almost any human activity. This, then, is my first secret to successful fishing.

1 A POSITIVE ATTITUDE

The person who expects success when he goes fishing will approach the sport with enthusiasm and take the time to do things right. Because he expects a strike, he is going to be sure that his lure is right, his knots are properly tied, and his landing net is ready for the big one.

It is interesting to watch the weekend "duffer" as he heads out onto the water, only half prepared. He feels defeated before he even starts out.

How do you get that positive feeling, that expectation of success? It comes partly from experiencing success and partly from learning from others, watching films on fish behaviour, and reading books like this one. Indeed, one of the objectives of this book is to provide some of that feeling of confidence.

2 ATTENTION TO DETAIL

This could also be called fastidiousness, fussiness, perfectionism, or any other of a number of terms for checking and double-checking every detail.

Successful fishing is not a laid-back sport. It requires that you do perhaps 20 or 25 little things all exactly right. Any weak link in the chain or a forgotten item will often result in getting skunked.

Any fisherman can stumble onto a fish by trolling around with his feet up while he sips a beer. And while this may give him a pleasant day in the sun, it won't bring consistent fishing success.

This may sound discouraging to those who look on fishing as a pleasant and relaxed outing. However, once you get in the habit of taking care of all the little details, they become almost automatic and fishing becomes even more pleasant, because now you are catching fish, which is the object of the exercise in the first place.

3   PERSISTENCE IS IMPORTANT

Successful fishing requires persistent effort. There is no substitute for spending time on the water, working your lures and working the likely fishing spots. The man who catches the most fish often spends the most hours with his line in the water.

Even the so-called experts get skunked more often than any of them will admit. Remember, if the fish aren't there, no one will catch them.

Even when there *are* fish in the area, often they just will not bite. My underwater camera shows that more than 90 percent of the fish that approach a lure turn away without striking. Biologists believe this is because the fish are not hungry. (And how many more don't even approach the lure because they feel satiated?)

One biologist told me that he believes a salmon will feed actively once a day for approximately 45 minutes, with another shorter feeding time of half an hour or less. The rest of the time is spent digesting the food.

We can often predict these feeding times with some accuracy, but other times we cannot. As Charlie Giuguet, a top biologist and expert fisherman, once told me, "Charlie, you just have to keep going out on the water."

4 KEEP RECORDS

Salmon and most marine creatures have a regular and predictable life cycle. Feeding habits, migrations, preferred habitat, and even depth and colour preferences vary with the time of year in a somewhat predictable manner.

For the past 25 years, I have kept a record of almost every salmon I have caught, listing all pertinent information in a diary or logbook. These records are kept in a manner that allows me to compare data for the same date or week of each year. For example, all of my catches for the third week in August over the past 25 years are listed together. This allows me an instant year-by-year comparison of my catches during that week.

After several years, a pattern emerged, which is extremely helpful for planning my fishing during that time of year. For instance, I may have noted that fish are likely to be at 100 to 130 feet below the surface, they prefer small spoons, and the "bite" usually takes place during the small, evening ebb tides.

Because baitfish have similar annual patterns, I also learn that a certain size of lure is most effective because it matches the natural growth cycle of the feed at that time of year.

Of course, the most important information such a diary provides is *where* the fish will be found. Seasonal migration patterns are extremely regular, and the salmon seem to show up almost like clockwork at the same spots during a certain week each year.

During spawning migrations, they are responding to their biological clock; the eggs and spawn ripen within the fish's body and push it toward its birthplace. Even during their active-feeding growth cycle, the salmon follow the baitfish (herring, anchovies, needlefish), which also move in a seasonal pattern as they follow the plankton and respond to water temperature and other factors. This means that concentrations of bait will show up at the same times and places each year and will surely be followed by the salmon.

You can use a spiral-bound notebook as a diary, or use one of the commercially available fishing logbooks. An example of a logbook is shown on pages 140-141.

5 BECOME A SPECIALIST

Fishing can become frustrating for anyone when the fish don't co-operate or when they just aren't there at all. This leads many fishermen to try virtually every lure in the tackle store in an attempt to catch fish by "throwing everything at them."

It often does make good sense to change your approach (see Secret 6), but it is almost impossible for anyone, especially a part-time fisherman, to master all of the intricacies of the various lures and fishing methods available today.

We all must specialize to some extent. Because my underwater camera works best when trolling, I have become a specialist in trolling and have even narrowed my lure choices. I use a lot of natural baits (herring, herring strip, anchovies), and I love to use bucktail flies with mother-of-pearl spinners when the coho are around. I use long, narrow spoons on sandy bottoms for needlefish and wider spoons when fishing in areas of small herring. I also troll with my downrigger most of the time.

A number of my fishing friends have moved almost exclusively to driftfishing, while others use certain flashers or dodgers in combination with hoochies, bait, or spoons. Only by specializing in certain techniques can you master the fine points that will improve your productivity.

Becoming a specialist also means specializing in certain fishing locations. It is far better to learn a few locations well than to rush around to a different spot every weekend and not learn those special "holding spots" for fish. Intimate knowledge of specific fishing areas is one of the most important secrets an angler can have. I know of a number of special drop-offs, places where tidal currents interact, and even flat sand bars where fish seem to congregate. I have learned of these special spots only from repeated trips to the same areas.

6 BE FLEXIBLE

While this may seem to contradict the secrets just outlined, it is important to be flexible enough to change your tactics when necessary. Don't follow too rigid an approach.

For instance, if you are trolling with herring strip and see fish being taken by other boats on flasher and hoochie, it makes sense to switch to another combination that might be more productive. Before changing lures, though, it is a good idea to make sure that you are fishing at the same depth as the other anglers. Often, getting to the right depth will allow you to catch fish on many different lure combinations.

The same holds true for location. You might be convinced that fishing a certain drop-off is most productive, then see fish "signs" (diving birds, seagulls, baitfish, or salmon jumping), which should lead you to investigate another spot.

I remember a dramatic incident at a fishing camp in Rivers Inlet, the fabled trophy-salmon area along B.C.'s northern coast. Shortly after noon, a new group of fishermen had flown in from Vancouver, eager to try their luck. Those of us who had been there several days had been fishing hard all morning and were preparing for an afternoon snooze.

The new arrivals were keen to get on the water and loaded their small putter boats with gear and bait for a mid-afternoon expedition. The "experienced" group watched with a chuckle as the newcomers took off. "They'll learn," we mused, "those fish aren't likely to bite in the lazy midday hours."

Two hours later we awoke from our naps to excited cries from the returning boats. Our eyes popped out as we watched three huge salmon being lifted from the boats and dragged to the weigh-in scales. Two of the salmon tipped the scales at over 70 pounds. They turned out to be the largest salmon taken in all of B.C. that year.

And they were taken between one and three in the afternoon, which all the conventional wisdom would say was a dead fishing time. For the next ten days there were no afternoon naps as the waters of Rivers Inlet were whipped to a froth all day long by every angler in camp! You just never know. You have to stay flexible.

On another occasion I was showing one of my underwater salmon-behaviour films to an audience in Campbell River, B.C., where many professional guides make a good living helping tourists catch fish. After the show, one of the guides approached me with a puzzled expression on his face. "Charlie," he said, "you showed those salmon grabbing the herring by the tail."

"Yes?" I replied.

"Well, they just don't do that," he muttered.

"Do you think I faked the pictures?" I said, smiling.

"I don't know what you did, but they just don't do that."

Here was a man, a professional, whose ideas were so fixed that he could not believe or accept a new idea, even with photographic evidence.

Chapter Two
PREPARING FOR A FISHING TRIP

Many anglers give no consideration at all to preparing for a fishing trip. They just get up in the morning, grab their clothes, rod, and tackle box, and take off for the boat. However, proper planning and preparation can have a substantial impact on fishing success.

7 USE QUALITY EQUIPMENT

Most of us who started fishing as children used hand-me-down equipment or maybe an inexpensive rod and reel bought through a promotional special. I'm sure we had a wonderful time fishing with this tackle, but, on the other hand, cheaply made gear can break down at critical moments, perhaps right in the middle of playing your biggest salmon of the season. Quality tackle gives pleasure and peace of mind.

I like to use nationally advertised brands, sold by a manufacturer who has a reputation to protect and is thinking long-term. The company wants its tackle to stand up to the tests of time and use so that you will buy it again yourself and recommend it to others. Some "off-brand" tackle is marketed for a quick buck. This is not to say that all unbranded tackle is of poor quality. However, you should either know the tackle or know the retailer who sells it to you.

8 USE A ROD WITH LIMBER TIP AND STIFF BUTT

I use a fibreglass rod between seven and a half and nine feet long. It has a sturdy butt and limber tip. The limber tip gives me the all-important shock-absorbing action that keeps a fast-running fish from breaking the line or tearing out the hooks during a sudden lunge. The sturdy butt gives me control when I need it, especially when leading a fish over the net.

Some of my charter customers were light-tackle extremists and would bring light fly rods to test their skill. After hooking a good salmon, they would enjoy ten to fifteen minutes of exciting action, then the fish would lie exhausted about twenty feet from the boat. Their light fly rods did not have enough strength in the butt to pull the exhausted fish to the net.

As a result, we would spend another ten to fifteen minutes trying to work the fish those last few feet while my other charter guests waited patiently for their turn to catch a fish. By the time the fish was in the boat, the hot fishing was often over. In my opinion, it would have been far better to enjoy the fish while it was active, then bring it to net and get on with the fishing. If an angler wishes to test his skill to this extreme, his fishing partners should fully understand the situation and be prepared to be spectators and not participants.

9 SINGLE-ACTION REEL GIVES MORE CONTROL

I like single-action reels better than the star-drag models, which use a slipping clutch. Single-action reels give me complete control of the fish, allowing me to apply varying amounts of drag with the palm of my hand and, more important, to *feel* the fish and enjoy every nuance of the fight.

Star-drag reels, on the other hand, rely on the clutch to slow down a running fish. Because each fish behaves differently, the drag adjustment is at best a compromise to handle an "average" fish (whatever that is!).

As a charter guide, I hosted guests who used star-drag reels and played their fish with no knowledge or feel of what the fish was doing. They just cranked furiously (and continuously) whether the fish was running out against the drag or coming toward the boat. They knew that eventually the exhausted fish would end up beside the boat, ready to be netted. This technique may put fish in the freezer, but the angler loses most of the fun and thrill of the catch. He might as well put a small motor on the reel and just wait to net the fish.

Worse still, many anglers adjust their clutch drags while playing a fish, often with disastrous results. When a stubborn fish just won't come in, the drag is progressively tightened until the fish is under control. As the straining fish is dragged to the net, it often makes one desperate run for freedom and breaks the line or tears out the hooks before the drag can be loosened.

Slipping-clutch reels do have some advantages. Older anglers or those with arthritic hands sometimes cannot master the alternate winding and palming technique of single-action reels and are more comfortable with star-drag reels. These reels also have a multiplying action (one turn of the handle means four turns of the reel), allowing the angler to keep up with a fish running fast toward the boat.

In the hands of a real expert, star-drag reels can be set with a loose drag and the angler adds a "thumbing" pressure to control the fish. This gives him some of the advantages of the single-action reel, plus the advantage of fast cranking when necessary.

However, reels with slipping clutches are more *mechanical,* more expensive, and require more servicing.

10 USE PLENTY OF LINE

I like to put plenty of line on my reel because it is surprising how far a big salmon can run. Fifteen hundred to 2,000 feet of twenty-pound-test line is about right for a five-inch single-action reel.

Incidentally, I think that twenty-pound-test line is adequate for playing any salmon. With a flexible rod tip, it is almost impossible to pull hard enough to break this line. It also allows you to get more line on the reel than using a heavier line does, and it has less friction in the water because of its smaller diameter.

Be sure to store your fishing reels out of direct sunlight, as ultraviolet light causes nylon line to deteriorate quickly. This is one reason why I swap the ends of my line at the end of the first season and discard it after the second.

11 CHOOSE THE RIGHT BOAT

Trolling is possible using virtually anything from a canoe or dinghy up to a yacht of 100 feet or more. Most trolling, however, is done using boats ranging in size from 12-foot cartoppers to 40- or 50-foot cruisers.

Cartopper fishermen usually mount a rod holder on each side of the gunwale and fish two rods, possibly using one downrigger for deep fishing. Larger craft can run four to six rods across the stern, and some use up to four downriggers. (Please check the current fishing regulations in your area for gear restrictions.)

The most important considerations for a good trolling boat are:

✧ Will it troll at an appropriate speed? Many high-powered, planing hull cruisers cannot be run slowly enough for proper lure action. This is especially true with a large single engine. Twin engines can be used to overcome this problem by trolling on one engine while using the "dead" propeller to help slow the boat. Boats with large engines can get slower speeds by using a small auxiliary outboard.

✧ Does it have a smooth-running engine? The head guide at a well-known fishing camp in Rivers Inlet kept a record of the fish caught from each of the boats and found that those with rough engines caught the least fish and those with the "sewing-machine smooth" engines were the most productive. A test in Washington State also found that commercial trolling vessels with well-tuned engines caught more fish than those powered by engines with misses or other noises or rattles.

12   ORGANIZE YOUR TACKLE BOX

When you are out on the water, it is invaluable to be able to find the right lure quickly rather than fumbling around in a disorganized mass of miscellaneous lures, line, swivels, etc.

Lay out the lures you are planning to use in a convenient spot. Consult your fishing diary and get the size, type, and colour of lures most likely to succeed. As a general rule, smaller lures are better for summer fishing, when baitfish are relatively small, and larger lures are better in the winter or in areas where mature herring gather.

Also, be sure you have such basic fishing tools as a pair of toenail clippers (clippers with a straight cutting face, not concave fingernail clippers), long-nose pliers, toothpicks (for herring strip), fishing knife, and a good hook sharpener.

13 PREPARE A CHECKLIST

If you prepare a checklist, you are less likely to forget some important item. The list should include such things as good polarized sunglasses (for reducing glare and seeing baitfish and other marine creatures under the water), tide book, marine chart, rods, reels, landing net, downrigger, rod holders, and any other items you will need.

Also include on your checklist such personal items as suntan cream, insect repellent, and appropriate clothing and rain gear.

14 CHECK YOUR BOAT

If you have a trailerable boat, you should also use a checklist to be sure that it is ready. This list would include such details as gas and oil for the motor, spare spark plugs (and other items in case of engine malfunction), life jackets, cushions, rod holders, downriggers, extra lead cannon balls, landing net, fish billy, gaff hook, boat fenders, depth sounder, mooring lines, and other related items.

15 DOES IT WORK?

It is wise to check the condition of each item. I have had fishing trips ruined because my depth-sounder battery was low or my downrigger wires were frayed.

16 PREPARE YOUR LURES

It is usually a good idea to tie up some of the lures you plan to use and store them in your tackle box or on your rod ahead of time. This saves critical minutes during those magic early-morning hours when you want to keep your gear working. You'll probably be more alert and under less pressure if you set up your gear the evening before rather than when you're out on the water. For instance, if leader lengths for a flasher or dodger are critical, you can take the time to get them exactly right. You can also tie up your herring-strip holders with fresh leaders and adjust them properly. And take the time to tie proper knots and test them by putting the hook around a solid object and giving a good hard tug on the line.

I usually leave successful lure combinations from one fishing trip just as they are for the next trip. However, it is important to check the leaders on these rigs for any nicks or frays.

You should also inspect the last ten to fifteen feet of your main fishing line for nicks and damage from attaching weights and downrigger clips or for abrasion from the line rubbing against the side of the boat. I make it a regular practice to snip off six to eight feet of my main line before every fishing trip, just to be sure.

It is also a good idea to have an extra rod rigged and ready to go so that if you lose some gear on a bottom hang-up, you can put out the extra rod and be fishing again immediately. An extra downrigger on board can save even more time if your wire breaks or kinks. The damaged gear can be repaired during a lull in the action and you are back to full preparedness again.

17 | HANDY CARDBOARD LINE HOLDERS

I have found that a small strip of heavy cardboard (approximately one by six inches) is a neat and effective holder for any lure that requires a leader. I use three-ply cardboard (usually available at liquor stores) with a slot cut in each end. Slide the bead-chain swivel through the slot at one end, then wrap the leader around the cardboard and stick the hook in the holder at one end. This little organizing trick has saved me many hours of untangling lures in a disorganized tackle box.

18 | PLAN A FISHING STRATEGY

There are always many unknowns during a fishing trip, but many things you will know the night before, and these should be used to plan a fishing strategy. For instance, you will know the tidal conditions from your local tide book, and you should also know which areas are most productive on these tides.

You will also have some idea of the forecast weather by listening to radio and television reports. Many areas have special marine reports that forecast wind and water conditions. These reports can be used to find a calm area to fish. Radio, TV, and newspaper reports also provide information on how the fish are biting in various areas. Some of these reports give extremely valuable information, while others are quite suspect. You will have to determine which ones give accurate information and which are designed to promote attendance at the local marina or boat rental.

Newspaper reports are often quite thorough, but tend to be somewhat out of date. Radio reports are often the most accurate, and many radio stations have cruisers on the water to give up-to-date information. All of these resources can be used to help plan a fishing strategy.

19 A PRIVATE NETWORK

Many anglers who fish in the same area share information. I make it a practice to call a number of local fishing friends and ask about their recent successes. You may find that your friends have been out on the water that very day and can give you information on your fishing spot, including important details on fishing depth, lure type, trolling speed, and even likely time for a bite.

20 PARTY FIRST, PAY LATER

Many anglers stay up late the night before a weekend fishing trip, often consuming copious amounts of liquor. When they get out on the water at 5:30 the next morning, they are often hung over, exhausted from too little sleep, and ill-prepared to make those on-the-spot decisions that will make the fishing day a big success. They are also unable to appreciate the joys of being on the water early in the morning. Each of us is issued only one body (our own Rolls Royce), which is designed to last a lifetime. We need to take good care of it to enjoy our fishing and all other aspects of healthy living.

Chapter Three
FINDING THE FISH

Obviously, the most important job for any angler is to find the fish. The greatest expert in the world, using the finest tackle and techniques, will be skunked if the fish aren't there.

21   GET OUT EARLY

Most of us aren't really keen to tumble out of bed in the dark in order to be on the fishing grounds at the crack of dawn, but it usually pays big dividends and is well worth the effort.

That jarring sound of the 4:00 a.m. alarm is just as tough on me as it is on anyone, but once I am up and moving, I love the early morning. I never get over that feeling of wonder at the beauty of dawn and the renewal of life and activity.

And there is no question that, all other things being equal, fishing is best during the first two hours of daylight. As far as we know, most fish do not feed at night and so are hungry in early morning. Sometimes fish migrate during the night and

COME AN' GET 'EM!!

arrive at their new location early in the morning, famished after their long overnight journey.

Baitfish are also on the move early in the morning. The plankton is often at the surface at night and moves down as the light brightens. The baitfish will be following it.

I had an interesting conversation with a biologist who worked on a mid-Pacific research team at the 180th degree longitude. This team was attempting to determine which salmon in the area were heading for Canada and the United States, and which for Japan and the Soviet Union.

This mid-ocean area is unique in that it has no tidal action to speak of. This eliminates the tide-change factor, which often affects fish-biting patterns along the west coast. Researchers found that with no tide factor, over 80 percent of the salmon were caught within the first two hours after daybreak. This was confirmed by all of the research boats over a long fishing period.

22 | FISH THE BACK EDDIES

Back eddies are those places where the tide or current moves around a point of land or other obstruction and forms an area of quiet water behind it. These spots are often good holding areas for salmon, which, like all fish, are basically lazy and don't want to work hard fighting a current. (In a way it's similar to stream fishing, where the most lucrative waters are often behind a big boulder or other quiet spoon in an otherwise rushing current.)

Plankton is swept into these back eddies, attracting euphausid shrimp, herring, and baitfish. This makes back eddies even more attractive for salmon and other game fish.

23 | FISH TIDE LINES

Tide lines or places with surface debris are often areas of mixing currents and are favoured by salmon, which usually lie on the quieter side of the tide line. Plankton and baitfish also gather here, sometimes hiding under floating logs or weeds. Migrating salmon often follow these tide lines even when they are far away from shore on their route to the spawning rivers.

One morning I was fishing for big, mature chinooks, close to a favourite shoreline of mine near Cowichan Bay on Vancouver Island. I watched in surprise as another boat, more than 100 yards from shore, hooked and landed a beautiful 30-pounder. I couldn't understand why that fish was so far from shore until I noticed a slight tide line moving out from a nearby point, pushed by a strong flooding tide. Following my "be flexible" rule (Secret 6), I started working that tide line in earnest and was rewarded with a fat chinook within half an hour.

24 | WATCH THE GULLS

Seagulls flying high above the water are like aerial spotter planes that can see the salmon and baitfish far better than we can from the water's surface. When you see gulls hovering above a certain area or dipping down into the water, it usually means they are near some fish.

When they gather in great flocks, squawking and squealing and diving into the water, they have found a bonanza, and the salmon are often underneath pushing baitfish to the surface.

25 | DIVING BIRDS TELL SECRETS TOO

Diving sea birds (often erroneously called diving ducks) are also an excellent sign of salmon. In fact, diving birds are often a more dependable indicator of salmon than seagulls.

LET'S CIRCLE HERE A WHILE, AND LURE THOSE GUYS AWAY FROM OUR FAVORITE FISH SPOT...

My experience is that murres, murrelets, and rhinoceros auklets (easily identified by the distinctive hump on their beaks) are the most reliable indicators of concentrations of baitfish and salmon. Grebes, cormorants, and others often turn out to be false alarms for me, but I know others who believe they are good indicators of fish.

Diving birds can also give you some tip-offs regarding the type of bait to use. Sometimes you will see them with the actual baitfish in their mouths. You can see if they are feeding on needlefish or on herring and get an idea of the approximate size of bait for matching with your own lure. You'll find that a pair of binoculars is helpful for studying diving birds.

We have some dramatic underwater footage of murres attacking herring in Juan de Fuca Strait. The murres swim down under the herring, always attacking from the bottom so that the herring are held trapped at the surface. They also "herd" the edges of the school like cowboys at an annual roundup.

Sometimes, however, only the birds are feeding on baitfish, and there are no salmon in sight. But even if salmon are not evident, it is wise to work the surrounding area, because non-feeding fish usually stay near the feed, close to their next meal for when they do get hungry.

26 FISH ABRUPT DEPTH CHANGES

Any steeply shelving area, whether it is against the shore or a change in depth offshore (near a shallow reef, for example), is an excellent holding ground for salmon. Chinooks especially seem to like these areas of abrupt depth changes. Mature, migrating chinook salmon will hug steeply shelving shorelines. I have caught many large chinooks (40 pounds and up) within ten to fifteen feet of almost vertical rock shorelines. Feeding immature chinooks will also concentrate tight against a bank in many instances.

Weed beds and kelp patches also provide an edge along which salmon will cluster. They will also hide in the kelp beds, ready to rush out and attack baitfish moving nearby.

27 WORK THE BOTTOM

Many salmon, especially chinooks, seem to hug the bottom except during active feeding periods or at the crack of dawn or evening twilight. I think that salmon (and all fish) like to be near some sort of reference point, whether it be a shelving shore or the bottom itself. Moreover, the bottom acts as a drag on water current so there is less movement and the salmon does not have to work so hard to maintain its position.

The bottom is also a rich source of food. On sandy bottoms, the needlefish (sand lance, candlefish) spend much of their time just above the sand or actually buried in it. Salmon hang close to the bottom in these sandy areas, on the lookout for a tasty meal.

Mud bottoms contain sea worms, while rocky bottoms have shrimp and prawns.

28 │ FISH CLOUDY WATER AND SHADED AREAS

Most fish seem to prefer water that is not "gin" clear and areas that aren't in direct sunlight. (This is one of the major problems we face with our underwater-camera research, as it is difficult to find salmon in clear, well-lit underwater environments.)

Where a muddy, freshwater river pours out over a saltwater estuary (and if the water is calm with no wave action to mix the fresh and salt water), there will sometimes be a definite dividing line between the murky water and the clear salt water underneath. We often see this on our underwater film footage as the camera drops beneath the turbid layer and bursts into clear water, almost like an aircraft descending from a fog bank.

Salmon often stay in the clear water under the murky surface layer, feeling safe from attack by surface predators. At places like Rivers Inlet in northern B.C., the rivers contain a colloidal suspension of glacial material, which cuts visibility to only a few inches. Lowering our underwater camera through this six- to ten-foot layer, we often poked out into the clear water and saw both pink and chinook salmon in sizable schools just beneath the covering layer.

29 │ LOOK FOR "ROLLERS" AND "JUMPERS"

This is the surest fish sign of all. You actually see the salmon as they roll on the surface or jump clear of the water. You can't get a more positive sign that fish are nearby, and you should fish these areas intensely.

Many people claim that rollers and jumpers will not strike; perhaps these folks have had frustrating experiences trolling through a school time and again with no success. And while it is true that rolling and jumping fish are often gathering near spawning areas and are thus less interested in active feeding, they *will* strike under certain conditions. (We will deal with these pre-spawning fish in Chapter Seven.)

Another excellent sign is fish "finning" on the surface. These fish are usually active feeders looking for baitfish or feeding on euphausid shrimp.

30 | WATCH FOR LANDING NETS

When the landing net comes out on a nearby boat, you know that someone has solved the mystery of finding the fish. By all means, learn what you can from this situation.

Close observation (with binoculars, if possible) can reveal many things to help improve your chances of success. Note the size of sinker as the fish is brought in, or look for the downrigger being retrieved to give you clues about depth. Some fishermen will even count turns as the successful angler cranks in his downrigger. Look also for the size and type of flasher or dodger and the size and colour of the lure in the fish's mouth as it is brought on board.

You can also watch the boat as it begins fishing again; observe its trolling speed and the area on which it concentrates. You can also watch the line being let out for additional clues on lure type and depth.

31 ASK OTHER FISHERMEN

Of course, the most direct method is to ask the successful fisherman for all the details. When I made this remark at one of my fishing classes, a voice from the audience shouted, "Yeah, and they'll lie like hell!" Sometimes they will, but I find that most anglers are willing to share information if approached tactfully.

After a fish has been landed, I often troll over to the successful crew, congratulate them on their success, and ask about the size of the fish. Usually they are delighted to talk about their fish and will often hold it up for me to admire.

I then follow up with questions on type of lure and fishing depth. These two bits of information, along with the area of catch (which you have observed already), give you enough details about his or her success.

32 | LISTEN TO YOUR RADIO

Many fishing boats are equipped with CB or VHF radios. Each fishing area has a preferred channel on which anglers exchange information on their catches and successful locations and lures. Some areas have become so competitive that this information is "coded."

You can also use your radio to ask for information on fishing conditions. I remember one plaintive call from a female angler who "just had to have salmon" for relatives who were coming for dinner that night. The response was instantaneous, and she got enough tips to fill a whole chapter of this book.

33 | A DEPTH SOUNDER IS CRUCIAL

This electronic tool is one of the most valuable any fisherman can have on board. It gives him underwater "eyes" with which to learn about bottom contours, location of salmon, and location of schools of baitfish. I have become so dependent on my depth sounder that once, when it quit in the middle of a holiday weekend, I stopped fishing, rushed back to town, and rousted my repairman from his backyard deck chair to make emergency repairs and get me back on the water.

I used to use a flasher sounder, but videograph sounders are now the norm. They give a detailed picture of the whole water column from surface to bottom, with plankton, baitfish, many species of fish, and even information on whether the bottom is sand, gravel, or rock and whether or not it has various types of seaweed on it.

I still use the video sounder primarily to keep track of the bottom for my downrigger control and to see concentrations of baitfish, which often show up quite clearly as a large ball, sometimes covering the whole screen. Many sounder experts can see individual fish by watching the inverted Vs moving across their screens.

Many anglers have sounders but do not use them properly. Sounders are sensitive instruments and will not give accurate information unless they are properly adjusted. Spend some time reading the instruction booklet and work with the sensitivity controls in particular, so you can get enough feedback to obtain good bottom and fish readings without all the unwanted "static" or "clutter," which can be confusing.

34 | TRY A TEMPERATURE PROBE

Great Lakes salmon anglers have used temperature devices for many years. The large freshwater lakes are quite stratified and have a thermocline where temperature change is quite rapid. Salmon and baitfish are often found in this area of temperature change. Locating it is probably the most important factor in Great Lakes salmon fishing.

I used to believe that Pacific Coast waters were cool enough and tidal mixing thorough enough that temperature was not a factor here. However, recent tests with temperature probes in conjunction with my underwater camera have convinced me otherwise.

During our underwater experiments, we attached a probe to the camera and began to record the temperature when we found salmon. Trolling at our normal depth of 30 to 35 feet, we found salmon at a water temperature of approximately 53°F (11.7°C). One morning we were trolling with no success and found that most of the other boats were also having no luck. Our temperature probe read 55°F (12.8°C). We lowered the camera until the temperature dropped to 53, and, almost magically, there were the salmon. They had moved another twenty feet deeper to find their preferred water temperature.

For the rest of the summer we used the temperature probe as our primary method of finding fish. We merely lowered the camera until we reached the 53-degree range and almost invariably found the salmon.. We plan further tests to find preferred water temperatures in spring and fall.

Incidentally, biologists tell us that fish will be completely inactive if the water drops below 39°F (3.9°C) and that any temperature above 55°F (12.8°C) will not be comfortable for salmon.

Chapter Four
BETWEEN YOU
AND THE BOTTOM

Trolling is probably the most popular method of salmon fishing throughout Canada and the United States, including the Great Lakes region of Ontario. Trolling has many advantages. It allows you to cover a great deal of water, exposes your lures to fish in many different areas, and gives those lures "action" and/or the lifelike or "wounded fish" appearance that entices salmon to strike.

35 FIND THE RIGHT DEPTH

Getting your lure to a depth where the fish are holding is probably the most important consideration in successful trolling. However, it is often difficult to *know* just how deep your lure is actually running. As you let out your line, it goes back in a parabolic arc with a gradually decreasing angle, so the line is most horizontal where it enters the water. The degree of this arc is dependent on many factors, including weight of lure and sinker, size and water resistance of the lure and flasher, line diameter, trolling speed and direction, and tidal condition.

In my opinion, downriggers are by far the best method to get your line down deep, get precision depth control, and still be able to play and land the fish on light tackle without dragging heavy weights or gear along with the running fish. Downriggers accomplish the latter task very well, but the following secrets will also help provide more depth per ounce of weight.

36 USE THIN-DIAMETER LINE

Thin-diameter line creates less drag in the water. The difference between even a fifteen- and twenty-pound line is quite apparent. The twenty-pound line (larger in diameter) will keep the line closer to the surface than will a fifteen-pound line with the same weight attached.

37 TROLL SLOWLY

This also minimizes drag, but often makes it difficult to get proper lure action. Try wobbling spoons, "flatfish" type lures, or specially rigged herring baits.

38 USE TRIP WEIGHTS

There are a number of gadgets on the market that allow you to drop a heavy lead weight as soon as a fish strikes. However, this requires a stiff, heavy rod to hold the line while trolling. Drop weights are also expensive to lose each time you get a strike, and sometimes the net result is only a dogfish or a big chunk of seaweed.

39 | USE PLANERS

These devices present a perpendicular surface to the line and drag it deep. They trip to a less resistant angle after a strike, but they also require a stiff rod for trolling.

40 | DOWNRIGGERS FOR PRECISE DEPTH

A downrigger is simply a large gurdy wheel holding 200 feet or more of wire line that is attached to a short rod extending over the side of the boat. A seven- to ten-pound lead weight drags the wire line to the desired depth, and a fishing line clipped to the wire line trips free when the fish strikes.

Get a good downrigger with an easy-to-read counter so you can measure fishing depth at all times. Using a downrigger with a depth sounder can be a deadly combination.

As I've already mentioned, salmon are often found close to the bottom and sometimes will take only lures trolled within a few feet of the bottom. By watching your depth sounder, you can crank the downrigger up and down over bottom contours, keeping your lure right in the strike zone at all times.

Electric-powered units, banned by the fisheries department for many years (because they were "too effective"), are now okay and are taking over the market. And no wonder! They allow you to retrieve the weight—now sometimes twelve pounds, even fifteen in extreme cases—by pushing a button while you play the fish.

When we used manual units, I would often be madly cranking the downrigger, usually two of them, while shouting instructions to my guest playing the fish. Sometimes the fish would arrive at the boat before the downriggers were safely out of the water, and fish-losing tangles would result.

I was instrumental in developing the Scotty downrigger, made in my home town of Sidney, B.C., and now a leading seller all over the world. This electric unit is among the most reliable in the business. Pardon the "plug," but I'm proud of my role in its development.

41 DOWNRIGGERS FIND "FISHY" DEPTHS

I often use two lines on each downrigger. This allows me to cover up to four depths at once while seeking out the productive fishing grounds.

I often continue to change depths on both downriggers, sometimes covering the whole spectrum down to 200 feet. Once the productive depth is found, the extra lines can be removed and both downriggers targeted to catch fish.

42 FLASH UP YOUR DOWNRIGGER

I dislike using flashers and dodgers as part of my fishing tackle because, in my opinion, it takes a great deal of the sport out of playing a fish. There is no doubt, however, that flashers and dodgers are effective in attracting fish, so I use a fishing technique that provides the benefits without the problems of dragging hardware on the fishing line itself. I hook my flasher or dodger on a four- to five foot, 80-pound nylon leader and attach it just above the downrigger weight with a bead-chain snap swivel. The flasher then rotates in the water (with no lure attached) and puts out an attracting flash and thumping vibration that brings fish to the area. Almost five times as many fish came to look at our underwater camera when we used a flasher as an attractor than when we did not.

We have also experimented with various forms of gang trolls (such as lake trolls, ford fenders, and other trout gear) as attractors, and these also work, but not nearly as well as a big rotating flasher.

Our fish behaviour studies, using a flasher and lure in the conventional arrangement, indicated that salmon sometimes were shy about coming too close to a flasher. This was especially true of large chinooks, which would sometimes cruise back and forth behind the lure and flasher, but would not approach to strike. Indeed, both commercial and sport fishermen have had greater success with big fish when they use long leaders (often five feet or more) between flasher and lure, a fact that confirms our findings. Using a flasher on a separate line attached to the downrigger will help overcome this problem.

43 | KEEP TENSION ON DOWNRIGGER WIRE

Downrigger wire carries an expensive cargo. The seven- to ten-pound cannon ball, snap swivel, flasher attachment, and release clip can add up to $15 or $20. Maintaining the wire in good condition will prevent loss.

The single most important way to protect downrigger wire is to keep some tension on it at all times. Never allow downrigger wire to go slack, even when it's stored on board the boat. I keep my cannon ball hooked on the downrigger even when mounting or dismounting it from the gunwale bracket and never lift the weight into the boat with slack line hanging over the side. Slack wire tends to twist on itself, and a serious kink will result when the line is tightened. When storing my downrigger, I wind the line tight to the pulley and hook the snap swivel back around the wire to hold it tight while in storage.

One more tip: Never drop your lead weight over the side on a slack wire. If you do, you will instantly learn one of the basic laws of physics: The momentum of a free-falling lead ball will snap the wire or snap swivel after only a short drop.

44 TAKE CARE OF YOUR DOWNRIGGER WIRE

If you get a kink or broken strands in the wire, it should be cut and respliced immediately. This is a relatively simple procedure and will make the wire as strong as new. Get some good wire cutters and crimping tools to do this job properly. Most sporting-goods stores carry them. If your downrigger wire breaks at the crimping sleeve, it means you have squeezed the crimps too tightly.

Even when used carefully, downrigger wires have a tendency to twist, so take time at the end of each fishing trip to untwist the wire. Simply put a light lead weight (perhaps one pound) on the snap swivel at the end of the downrigger wire and troll it in deep water. This will relieve the line of any strain and twist.

Incidentally, downrigger wire can be stressed by being pulled over too small a pulley at the end of the downrigger arm. The larger the diameter of this pulley, the less stress on the downrigger wire itself. Keep this in mind when deciding which unit to purchase.

All downrigger wire is made of stainless steel, but it does seem to pick up rust spots from repeated exposure to salt water. There are many grades of stainless steel, and apparently downrigger wire is not quite as "stainless" as it could be. You can minimize the damage saltwater exposure causes by periodically applying a rust preventative such as WD-40, which will drive out moisture trapped in the wire and protect and lubricate it.

45 | ROUND WEIGHTS ARE BEST

Downrigger fishing originated in the Great Lakes area of the United States, and most downriggers developed there come with fancy, streamlined weights with release clips attached right to the weights themselves. These weights are pretty flashy and probably have a lot of sales appeal, but in my opinion they are not as good as a simple round ball. The whole idea is to get as much depth per ounce of weight as possible, a feat best accomplished by exposing the minimum amount of surface area to the water, thereby reducing the friction drag that keeps the weight from reaching maximum depth.

Basic physics tells us that a spherical or ball-shaped weight will enclose the most weight in the least surface area. This means that it is the most efficient and, luckily, only about half as expensive as some of the fancy streamlined weights.

I tested this theory near my home at Patricia Bay on Vancouver Island. I lowered two downrigger weights of identical poundage (one round, one streamlined) to an exact depth of 100 feet, then trolled from deep water onto a sandy shelf. Inevitably, the round ball hit bottom first, meaning, of course, that it was trolling deeper than the streamlined Great Lakes weight.

Some advocates of streamlined weights say that round balls will spin and cause the wire line to twist. Sometimes this is true, but the spin can be stopped by simply adding a "pigtail" to the downrigger ball. To do this, drill a small hole into the side of the ball and insert about ten inches of quarter-inch polypropylene line, then secure it with some one-inch galvanized nails. This will keep the ball from spinning and is also handy for lifting it on board.

(SAME LENGTH OF LINE)

46 | AVOID BOTTOM HANG-UPS

One thing you will learn very quickly when using downriggers is that bottom hang-ups can come suddenly, unexpectedly ... and be very expensive. Indeed, learning to fish with downriggers is somewhat like learning to drive a car. In that regard, I remember concentrating so much on co-ordinating my hand and foot-pedal movement that I sometimes forgot to watch where I was going. In the same way, getting used to co-ordinating downriggers, lures, fishing rods, and rod holders often means that you forget to watch the depth sounder or where the boat is heading. This will likely result in a few bottom hang-ups and lost tackle before good old trial and error teaches you to be more alert.

It is a good idea to learn basic downrigger techniques over a sand or mud bottom. This allows you to hit bottom without losing any tackle. Sometimes you will gather up some seaweed and debris, but at least the gear will come back more or less intact. Rocky bottoms are a different story entirely.

The only way to avoid bottom hang-ups is to know the water thoroughly, use marine charts, and—most important—

use a good depth sounder. Keep it turned on the entire time you are fishing and monitor it continuously.

You can also use shore markers, or "gunsight marks," to plot your direction of travel. For instance, you can keep yourself on course along the edge of a drop-off by lining up an object on shore with another object farther inland. This will give you an exact line to follow.

An "anti-snag" device on your downrigger weight will also warn you of imminent contact with the bottom. This is simply a piece of stiff wire (coat-hanger wire or heavier) that is attached to the downrigger ball (or actually inserted in a hole drilled in the weight) and extends below it. When the wire hits bottom it telegraphs a signal to the surface, warning you to raise the weight—quickly. It works much like the spring devices attached to car fenders to indicate when you are getting too close to the curb.

47 | HANDLING BOTTOM HANG-UPS

Despite taking the precautions just described, everyone gets caught on a bottom hang-up sooner or later. The procedure for handling this situation will vary according to the prevalent tide and wind conditions. For instance, if you are fishing in a relatively quiet area with little tidal movement and no wind, you can simply put the boat in neutral and reverse or circle around to work the weight free of the bottom. In this situation, it is usually best to trip the fishing lines and reel them in as quickly as possible (as well as any other downriggers that are not hung up on the bottom). Otherwise, stopping the boat will allow the rest of the gear to settle on the bottom, resulting in even more hang-ups.

The more common situation is when there is some tidal movement and/or some wind, which makes it more difficult to stop or change boat direction fast enough to free the weight quickly. When the weight hits a rocky bottom, I find it best to jerk hard on the downrigger crank in an effort to jolt the weight loose, rather than "babying" the weight by loosening the gurdy. Loosening the line often allows the weight to settle deeper into a rocky crevice, making it almost impossible to work loose, especially against a wind or tide. Jerking the weight hard will sometimes cost you the lead (the snap swivel opens to release the trapped weight), but it will usually save the rest of the gear. Trying to work it loose will often result in losing flasher, lure, release clip, and often a good chunk of downrigger wire to boot.

By keeping a close watch on the downrigger wire, you can react immediately upon hitting bottom and pull the weight free in most instances.

48 SET DOWNRIGGER LINES PROPERLY

To minimize tangling when putting out downrigger lines, a definite procedure should be followed. The boat should be moving in a straight line at trolling speed. (Try to anticipate the movement of other boats so you won't have to turn unexpectedly in the middle of putting out the gear.) Lower the downrigger ball into the water, then strip out fifteen to twenty feet of line from the reel and attach the line to the release clip. Check lure action to make sure that it is working properly. Snap the release clip onto the downrigger wire and lower away.

If you are using two lines on one downrigger, lower the gear to the second set of line markers and repeat the procedure for the second fishing line before lowering to the desired fishing depth. It is desirable to have a downrigger with a clutch-brake system, which allows a smooth, easy lowering of the gear and eliminates half the work. You don't have to crank it down as well as up. When turning the boat you must be careful that the downrigger wire does not catch in the propeller. This can be more of a problem if you're using a small auxiliary outboard on one side of the stern, since only a small turning angle will bring the wire close to the propeller. A stiff wind from the side or fishing in a cross-tide can cause the same problem, forcing the downrigger wire under the boat and toward the propeller. One way to counter this situation is simply to reach over the side with a gaff or boat hook and lift the wire clear of the propeller.

Sharp 180-degree turns should also be avoided, especially when using multiple downriggers in deep water. Downrigger wires can wrap around themselves in this situation and become a real mess to untangle. I remember fishing a big tide rip in Sansum Narrows when we got our downrigger wires twisted together under the boat, a mess that took almost an hour to untangle. We lost one downrigger ball and, more important, missed the best fishing of the day.

49 | WATCH DOWNRIGGER PULLEY, NOT ROD TIP

Because your fishing rod is attached firmly to a release clip on the downrigger wire, any fish strike is transmitted immediately up the wire to the downrigger pulley. In fact, the downrigger pulley is a more reliable indication of a strike than the rod tip itself.

The line between the rod and the release clip is subject to fouling with weed and also has a strong friction drag, which changes as it passes through the propeller wake or a tide line.

These influences can often cause the rod top to bounce, giving false indications of strikes. It is much better to watch the end of the downrigger pulley for the telltale jiggle (or resounding thump) that indicates a strike.

Even the tiniest fish will give a few good tugs before giving up and just trailing along on the lure. If you are watching the wire at all times, you will see this movement and be able to remove the fish. Otherwise, you might drag the little thing around for hours, drowning the fish and eliminating any possibility of a bigger strike.

50 | ELECTRIC-MODEL TECHNIQUES

The newer electric models have a much stiffer arm, and the arm movement from a small strike is more difficult to see and less likely to cause an alarm bell to sound. It is still possible, but a better approach is to use release clips with a twelve- to eighteen-inch leader between wire attachment and the place where the line is clipped on. This leader allows the fishing line to move very actively, and the rod tip will move a foot or more when a fish strikes. Even a tiny fish strike or weed hang-up can be seen if you are watching the rod tip. These release clips also allow you to clip and unclip line from inside the boat without leaning out to the end of a long pulley arm.

51 HAND-HOLD WIRE OR USE ALARM BELL

I often sit on the gunwale of the boat, holding the downrigger wire between my fingers while watching the other downrigger on the opposite side of the boat. I sense the slightest strike through my fingers, and I seldom miss a strike using this procedure. If I have several fishermen aboard, I often assign each one to hold a downrigger wire.

Some anglers have designed alarm bells that they attach to the end of their downrigger pulley arms. These alarms come in various configurations, but most use an extension arm that magnifies any movement of the downrigger pulley and gives more action to the bell. Some of these bells work well, but others ring all day long, making them useless for detecting strikes and driving the fisherman crazy with the noise.

If, however, you mount the bell on its side, the clapper will be activated only when the downrigger arm is jerked by a strike or bottom hang-up.

Chapter Five
TROLLING TECHNIQUES

I believe that trolling with a downrigger is *the* most effective trolling technique, and I use this method 90 percent of the time. The only exception is trolling bucktail flies on the surface for coho salmon. This is probably the most exciting and sporting way to catch salmon, but surface-feeding coho are only available for short periods during the season.

The following trolling techniques can be used with or without downriggers, as the same general principles apply.

52 | CHOOSE THE RIGHT LURE

A group of anglers working a school of fish can usually catch them on a number of different lures, but some general principles apply no matter what they use. Note the following:

✧ Match the size and shape of natural bait in the area. Fish are more easily tempted into striking if your lure looks like the natural feed they are trying to catch. They are conditioned to seek out the wounded baitfish, so the more your lure looks like that particular baitfish, the more likely the strike.

✧ Small spoons such as Point Defiance, Kripple K, and Tom Mack match the general shape of herring. (The spoon should get larger as the season progresses to match the bait's growth.) Needlefish concentrations, found over sandy bottoms, are increasing all along the northwest coast, and the use of long, narrow spoons is increasing rapidly. Such names as needlefish nailer, needlefish troller, and Koho Killer are popular. Thin hoochies, squirts, and bucktail flies also can be used to imitate needlefish. Hoochies and bucktails also imitate squid, a major source of food for salmon and other fish.

✧ Almost any type of spoon can be made much more effective by adding a tiny bit of bait to the trailing hook. It can be tiny indeed, perhaps only one-sixteenth of an inch wide and a half-inch long. If this bit of bait dampens lure action, use a piece of skin or even a tiny piece of plastic hoochie tail to give added action.

53 | LARGE BAITS CATCH TROPHY FISH

A major exception to the foregoing is when you are fishing for trophy-sized salmon. Our underwater-camera tests showed quite conclusively that large salmon prefer a large bait, even when the natural feed in the area is small. Moreover, biologists tell us that this ties in with a "conservation of energy" behaviour practised by large predators of many species of fish and animals. Salmon become lazier and wiser as they grow larger. They don't want to use a lot of energy chasing small bait when they can gulp down one large one.

This brings to mind an interesting and illuminating experience I had while visiting New Zealand with my family during a once-in-a-lifetime South Pacific holiday. We chartered

HURRY UP! I'M REALLY HUNGRY!!

a fishing boat skippered by one of the top guides in New Zealand's Bay of Islands. This guide had more than 40 years' experience, including some time as a crew member on the boat used by Zane Grey on his famous fishing trips many years ago. The guide told us that New Zealand marlin were not large; the biggest he had ever caught weighed some 275 pounds.

Before fishing we jigged some kahawai as bait. These tuna-like fish averaged about two pounds, and the boys really enjoyed catching them. Suddenly Kevin hooked and landed a huge eight-pound specimen, which the guide wanted to throw back. Kevin insisted we keep it; it was the largest of the day, so we threw it into the bait tank with the others.

Later we ran into a school of hammerhead sharks, and they gobbled all of our bait. The guide told us we should go to artificial lures. I suggested we try the eight-pound kahawai still in the bait tank. He chuckled and said that they *never* used bait even half that large. However, I insisted, so he rigged the bait and trolled it over the stern. Within twenty minutes we hooked a huge marlin, battling it for several hours. It weighed over 400 pounds and won us the award for largest marlin taken in New Zealand waters that year.

I believe that our success was more than luck. We were using bait two or three times as large as that used by other boats in the area, and that grandfather marlin knew what he wanted.

54 | ATTACH THE LURE CORRECTLY

Most quality lures are designed with great care to give superior fish-catching action when trolled properly. One of the most important details in this regard is balance. Your leader should be tied directly to the lure itself to maintain the balance designed into the lure by the manufacturer.

You should never hook a snap swivel or other device to the leading edge of the lure because this could completely alter its balance and action. It may be a bit more convenient to hook lures this way, but you are defeating the whole purpose. You can, however, use a snap swivel between the leader and main line. I use a bead-chain snap swivel at the end of my main line and hook another swivel to the end of my leader. This allows me to change lures quickly when leaders are already attached to them.

The action of a plug can also be changed dramatically by the position of a knot tied to the eye in front of the lure. Tying the knot snug at the top of the eye will make the lure dig deeper than tying it to the centre or bottom of the eye. Many expert plug fishermen use knot positions as a major adjustment in controlling plug action.

55 TIE A GOOD KNOT

More fish are lost because of poor knots than for almost any other reason. Some anglers just don't know how to tie a good knot and others are just too careless to do it properly.

Several manufacturers of monofilament line have their own knots, which they recommend for their particular brands. However, most knots are a variation of the jam knot, blood knot, or clinch knot. This last knot is tied by wrapping the line around itself several times and then looping it back through the gap between the hook and the first loop.

The following illustration shows two of the knots I like best.

56 LUBRICATE LINE BEFORE TIGHTENING KNOTS

Nylon line can score, burn, or fray when pulled tight. It is important to wet the line (with a bit of saliva) before pulling the knot tight. This lubricates the line and cools it a bit, minimizing the scoring problem.

57 | CHECK LURE ACTION

This simple tip seems so obvious, but it is amazing how many fishermen are so eager to get their lure in the water that they just throw it over the side and strip out line without bothering to see whether it is working properly.

What is proper action? Most lure manufacturers enclose detailed instructions in their packages and usually give tips on proper action for each lure. By all means read these instructions thoroughly and take advantage of the manufacturers' research and experience. After all, they are successful only if you catch fish, and their instructions should give you the best information possible.

Checking lure action beside the boat will also tell you when an *unusual* action turns out to be productive. Sometimes I have been unable to get my herring strip working "normally" but have lowered it down anyway rather than change to a fresh bait. Sometimes I have been startled by a vicious strike almost immediately. By remembering the unusual lure action, I have duplicated it—and learned a whole new fishing secret.

58 | CHOOSE LIKELY DEPTHS

We covered this point pretty thoroughly in the section on downriggers, but for non-downrigger trollers there are two other basic patterns to consider:

⬧ If you expect the fish to be at shallow depths, put two shallow lines on each side of the boat and a deep line down the middle.

✧ If you expect the fish to be deep, hang two deep lines over the side of the boat and a shallow line down the middle.

When fishing with downriggers I often put a single light line right over the stern to pick up any shallow feeders, especially any coho that might be investigating the propeller wash.

Be sure to count the pulls as you let out your line. (A "pull" is usually about eighteen inches and is done by grasping the line at the reel and pulling toward the first rod guide.) If you catch a fish at 40 pulls, you can return to the same depth just as you would with downriggers, although the pull method is not quite as accurate.

59 CHECK YOUR GEAR REGULARLY

I make it a practice to inspect my lures every 15 to 30 minutes, whether I am getting strikes or not. This allows me to ensure that my lures are not fouled with weed or jellyfish. It also exposes the lures to fish in the complete column of water, from the surface to the deepest fishing line. Often a salmon will grab the lure as it is being reeled in or let out.

If I get a strike when bringing in the line, I will often fish shallower or faster, since this could indicate a shallow fish or a fish that simply wants to chase a faster-moving lure.

Of course, the opposite is true too, and if you get a strike when lowering your tackle, this may mean that the fish like a slower-moving lure, and your trolling speed can be adjusted accordingly.

60 | FOLLOW THE FISH DOWN

At the crack of dawn salmon are often feeding very close to the surface, usually on baitfish, which are feeding on surface plankton. As the sun moves higher in the sky, the plankton, baitfish, and salmon tend to move deeper.

While fish tend to feed more actively in the first two hours after daybreak, they will often bite well into the day if you are willing to follow them deep enough.

I often encounter a good early-morning bite on top of a 50-foot shelf near my home in Saanich Inlet. When the "bite" goes dead I usually move offshore to the adjacent deeper water, where I will find that the fish are often still in a striking mood.

I can remember one occasion when I had four fishing students on board and we caught four nice salmon on top of the shelf. We continued to follow the fish down the edge of the shelf, lowering our downriggers deeper and deeper. We caught our limit of twenty salmon that morning, most of them over 100 feet down, and the last one (a lovely fourteen-pounder) was taken just before noon with the downrigger depth counter reading 275 feet. Incidentally, that fish swam straight to the surface (my fishing student could hardly reel in fast enough) and put up a spectacular fight on the surface. Salmon must have a marvelous internal mechanism to adjust to such tremendous changes in pressure.

61 | FISH A ZIGZAG PATTERN

Watching salmon follow lures behind our underwater camera, we discovered that they will sometimes follow the lure for long periods without striking. Changing direction, however, will sometimes trigger a strike, and indeed, many anglers say they often get strikes while making a turn.

Fisheries-department tests off the west coast of Vancouver Island used commercial trollers to find ways to increase productivity. One of their most significant findings was that catches were higher when boats fished a zigzag pattern rather than trolling in a straight line.

I often fish along a tide line where two opposing currents mix, usually fishing back and forth across this dividing line with considerable success.

When fishing bucktail flies, I make very sharp turns of up to 90 degrees. I troll straight ahead for perhaps 100 yards, then turn the wheel hard over to make a sharp change in direction. This causes the outside fly to whip ahead quickly and the inside fly to stop dead in the water. These dramatic changes will often trigger an excited coho into a smashing strike.

62 | FISH IN ONE DIRECTION

Most fishermen don't know about the important changes in lure action (with relation to tide or wind) that take place when they change direction. Our underwater camera revealed some interesting findings. For instance, trolling with the tide, our lures would often speed up as we went deeper. This is because surface water moves faster than deeper water, pushing the boat ahead faster relative to the lure.

The opposite happened when we trolled against the tide. We often had to advance the throttle two or three times as fast as anticipated in order to keep the same trolling action on the lures. Sometimes 500 revs on the motor worked with the tide, but we would have to go to 1200 or 1500 revs to get the same action against the tide.

Without access to a camera, it would be virtually impossible to get the same lure action in both directions. And even if you did, you might find that the fish still strike only while you're trolling in one direction.

If you get strikes trolling in one direction (usually with the tide), it is usually best not to try to troll back against the tide. Just pull in the gear and run back to the starting point.

63 | DOWN WITH THE TIDE, BACK IN THE EDDY

As already noted, salmon tend to hang out in back eddies. Thus it is usually most productive to fish down with the tide just at the outside edge of the eddy, then around and up with the back-eddying tide so that you have the water pushing you along throughout the whole process. If you fish against the tide (in the opposite direction around the circle), you will be fighting the current all the time and probably end up standing still relative to the bottom. If there are many boats fishing an eddy, they will usually fall into a circular pattern like that just described, and you will have to follow this pattern anyway to avoid collisions.

64 FISH ACROSS THE TIDE

As already mentioned, fishing with and against the tide is often productive, as is fishing in back eddies along the tidal flow direction. However, as noted in Secret 6, remaining flexible and trying new things often produces unexpectedly good results. This is sometimes true of fishing across the tide, perpendicular to the direction of flow.

During one of our filming expeditions, we were working back and forth along a rocky shoreline, with very spotty results. Twenty or 30 other boats were following the same pattern, also with no success. I spotted what looked like a tide line about 300 yards from shore. Rather than haul in the underwater camera and all the other gear, we decided to troll across the tide toward this new location. Much to our surprise, we began to take fish in the intermediate area between the shore and the distant tide line, fishing across the main tidal flow.

We have repeated this pattern on several occasions and have had good results at least 50 percent of the time. There seems to be no logical explanation for this except that we were fishing new water untapped by the other boats in the area. Of course, trolling across the tide is only possible in areas where there is not heavy fishing pressure. Otherwise, you will be constantly dodging other boats and their trailing lines.

If you get a strike when fishing across the tide, turn into the tidal flow rather than downstream when attempting to get back to the productive spot. An upstream turn will put you right back where you want to be, while a downstream turn may result in a long struggle to work your way back against the tide.

65 DON'T TROLL INTO THE SUN

Fisheries research describes a test at a trout hatchery that fed its stock floating food pellets. It was found that the trout always attacked the pellets on the sunny side, often driving all of the pellets to the far side of their pond. This directional striking behaviour was most pronounced in early morning or late evening. The trout attacked the pellets with the sun at their back, just like the fighter pilots in the First and Second World Wars.

After studying this data, we watched our monitors more closely as salmon approached the underwater test lures. We noticed immediately that there was a difference in their behaviour when we trolled directly toward the sun. They would still approach and follow the lures, but a much smaller percentage actually struck. Often they would strike soon after we made a turn away from the direction of the sun. We too found this situation most pronounced in early morning and late evening.

We realized that we had often trolled toward the sun during our underwater tests because it put the best light on the lures and on the salmon themselves, giving us better light for our TV pictures. But the salmon obviously couldn't see the lures as well because they had the sun in their eyes. Our underwater camera had discovered another secret that is just plain common sense. Like airplane pilots and automobile drivers, salmon don't like steering into the sun.

66 USE THE GEARSHIFT

Mechanics tell me that this technique can be hard on the engine, but it can be effective for certain fishing situations. Once, a friend who was having no luck asked me to come along to find out what was wrong. It was obvious that he was trolling too fast, but his high-speed inboard would not troll down. His heavy downrigger weight streamed out behind the boat at quite an angle, robbing him of needed depth and forcing his lures to whirl wildly.

I suggested we put the motor out of gear and let the downrigger and lures swing down to a more vertical position. Within fifteen seconds we were rewarded with a vicious strike and soon after had an eight-pound chinook in the landing net.

We used this technique for about two hours and ended up with our limit of twelve nice chinook, up to fourteen pounds each. It would take about 45 seconds after putting the motor in neutral for the downrigger to reach a vertical position, then we would put the motor back in gear for two or three minutes until the 150 feet of wire were streaming behind again.

This technique allowed us to troll the lure through a wide range of depths and also changed the lure action. In this instance, the fish were very deep, and they struck as the lure fluttered down to the bottom of their range, or just after we put the motor back in gear.

You can use the same technique without a downrigger, sometimes getting even more dramatic results. Trolling with six or eight ounces of weight and a long line, the lures will drop down in a long arc between full trolling configuration and vertical. This will cover an even wider range of depths.

67 | VARY YOUR SPEED

Normal trolling speed is the speed at which your lures have the right action. Most lures, however, can be adjusted to give proper action at several different speeds. You can adjust the degree of bend in a spoon, change the knot position on a plug, and adjust the hook position on various bait hookups to give proper action at different speeds.

If you are not getting any strikes at your normal trolling speed, increase your speed 25 to 50 percent and adjust the lures to work correctly at this speed. You may be surprised at the results. Commercial trollers move much faster than most sport boats and have consistent success because their lures are "tuned" for these faster speeds. Faster speeds also allow you to cover more water, thereby exposing your lures to more fish.

I recall one mid-October morning when we fished for coho in Cowichan Bay on Vancouver Island. Coho were jumping all over the bay, but none of the 75 boats there were having any success at all. Knowing that coho sometimes like a very fast lure, I decided to test my faster trolling theory to the extreme. I advanced the throttle until the bow of the boat actually began to rise up toward a planing position. Just as I was beginning to feel ridiculous, one of my rods snapped back with a force that almost jerked it clear of the rod holder. The reel screamed at an adrenalin-pumping pitch I had never heard before and haven't since. After a spectacular fight, we landed a beautiful twelve-pound, hook-nosed fish that must have had a twisted neck from the force of the strike.

It can also be productive to troll much slower than normal. This is especially true in areas where chinook salmon are "holed up" and not feeding actively. In this kind of situation, it is important to give the fish the maximum amount of time to look over your bait as it wobbles or rolls slowly past its nose.

As a general rule, I like to troll relatively slowly during periods when the fish are not feeding actively, but speed up considerably during the "bite" (when they are actively seeking food). A hungry fish will be triggered by a fast-moving bait, while a fish that is resting or digesting its food is not likely to be motivated to chase it.

68 | VARY LINE LENGTH

Normally I put my lure about 12 to 15 feet back from my downrigger wire, but sometimes I will place it as much as 20 to 40 feet back, especially if I'm trolling in relatively shallow water. In clear water you can put the lure farther back; shallow lines can also be back farther to get them away from the boat and propeller disturbance.

If the water is murky, I want the lure to be relatively close to the flasher (rotating on its own line at the downrigger ball) because the fish will be attracted to the vibrating thump but won't see the lure if it is too far away. You can put the lure as close as six or seven feet from the release clip in this situation.

When fishing without downriggers—and especially when using surface-running bucktails—both extremes work well. I often troll my bucktails only 20 to 30 feet behind the boat, and sometimes right in the prop wash, where coho are attracted by the bubbles. This is most effective in areas where the coho are still feeding actively.

In estuary areas, on the other hand, the fish are sometimes more easily spooked and won't come near the boat. One morning off Cherry Point near Cowichan Bay, we saw one boat take three fish in a row while the other 50 boats were catching nothing but eelgrass. I pulled alongside and asked all the usual questions about lure, size, and colour, but it turned out we were already doing everything correctly. Only as we pulled away and watched him strip out line did we realize that he was fishing almost 200 feet back from his boat, while we were only 60 feet back. Obviously, the fish were extremely wary of all the boat activity. When we matched his long line, we began taking fish almost immediately.

69 USE GUNSIGHT MARKS TO PINPOINT LOCATION

Salmon are often found in tightly bunched schools covering an area of perhaps 50 feet in radius. This is a tiny segment in the vastness of most fishing areas.

Once you locate the fish, by all means mark the spot as precisely as possible. In the excitement of a strike it's often difficult to remember your position, but taking good marks can pay big dividends by getting you back to the hot spot.

Most "high-liner" fishermen use range markers or "gunsight" marks to pinpoint their location. The gunsight-marks technique was taught to me by Rhys Davis, the bait-fishing guru who developed the famous Strip Teaser line of lures. He used it his whole life. (He passed away recently at the age of 93, and enjoyed fishing right to the end. Fishing is good for your health!)

Most weekend fishermen believe it is good enough to look toward an approximate shore location or try to line themselves up between two markers on opposite shores. Neither of these methods is very accurate, as a 10-degree error in either direction can put you as much as 900 feet off the correct spot, even if you are only a half-mile offshore.

The correct method is to line up two objects on the same side of the boat, one behind the other (a rock on the shoreline with a tall tree behind it, for example). Lining up two sets of range markers at approximately 90 degrees to each other will give you two intersecting "lines" and a position exactly over the spot where you hooked the fish.

Your first attempts to fix these marks will probably be awkward and inaccurate, but you'll be amazed at how quickly you will learn to take good marks, especially when you reap the rewards of such a procedure.

After marking the spot you will probably want to put the motor in neutral and enjoy playing and landing your fish. You can then circle around, line up one set of marks, then troll until you cross the other set.

Of course, you will also want to locate the fish in the third dimension (depth), so it is important to note the reading on your downrigger before retrieving it. If you were trolling without a downrigger, you will need to remember how much line (the number of pulls) was out.

70 USE GPS

The electronics revolution has brought a new tool for pinpointing a location: GPS (Global Positioning System). The push of a button will allow you to return to an exact fish location, or to that hot spot for crabs or prawns. It is a feature available in most of the depth sounders on the market today. (I use a Furuno, a bit pricey for some wallets, but it has all the bells and whistles.)

71 MARK LOCATION WITH FLOATING OBJECT

An alternate method of marking a location is to throw a floating object over the side of the boat immediately after getting a strike. This can be a seat cushion, an empty bleach bottle (preferably with a one-pound weight to minimize wind drift), or any other appropriate floating object. This procedure works well when the water is relatively calm and the floating object is not hidden in wave troughs. It is also effective for marking the location of surface-feeding coho when the tide is running, as the floating object will move with the school as it drifts along in the tide.

I've seen people throw beer bottles or trash to mark a location, but this is just plain littering. Let's do everything we can to maintain our environment and upgrade the image of fishing and fishermen.

72 | FINDING THE BIG SCHOOL

When I was a fishing-charter guide in the late 1950s, I was out on the water almost every day, and I learned a lot of special tricks to help me stay with the main body of fish as it moved from one location to another. On many occasions I would have several "hot" days, catching limits for the entire party. Sometimes we would "limit out" for two parties in one day—with four or five persons in each party and a five-fish limit, we might take 30 or 40 fish. Then one morning I would return to the same spot and begin catching smaller runt fish or fish with some deformity (usually a torn mouth from a previous hookup or an injury from a seal or other predator). I soon learned that this meant the main school had started to move to another location. The stragglers couldn't keep up and remained behind to pick up the leftovers.

When I began to catch these undersized fish, I would immediately begin to explore anywhere from a few hundred yards to a quarter of a mile in either direction in search of the main body of fish at the next "holding" spot.

73 | SANDY-BOTTOM TECHNIQUE

When fishing on a sandy bottom, you can use your downrigger effectively to get the lure right on the bottom where salmon are literally picking the baitfish (candlefish, sand lance) right out of the sand. Use a long, narrow metal spoon such as the

Kobo Killer, Koho King, or Needlefish lure, attaching it 25 to 30 feet back from the downrigger release clip.

Lower the downrigger quickly and smoothly (a good clutch brake handles this well). Jerky, intermittent lowering of the downrigger can cause the leader to foul with the flasher. When the downrigger ball touches bottom, crank up one or two turns and you are ready to fish.

The weight of the metal spoon and the distance behind the release clip allows it to ride just above the sand. You can also add a tiny weight (perhaps a half-ounce) on the main line near the swivel to the leader.

You will need to check your lure frequently, since there is a great deal of lettuce weed and other debris on sandy bottoms, and fouled lures don't catch many fish. You should also keep probing for the bottom by lowering the downrigger every few minutes to ensure that you are still riding just above the sand. Your depth sounder will help determine when to lower or raise the downrigger weight.

74 | BIG CHINOOK PREFER ROCKY SHORELINES

Large chinook salmon often hang out along steeply shelving, rocky shorelines, sometimes right tight against the rocks. They seem to lie in wait like an animal in its lair, ready to ambush passing baitfish.

They won't travel very far to strike a passing lure, so you must get close to the rocks themselves. I have found it effective to troll straight toward the shore or reef and then turn sharply when the sounder warns of the steeply shelving bottom. This will swing your lures into the chinooks' territory, often triggering a strike just after making the turn. This is a risky business, though, since you can hang up the downrigger and all the gear if you cut it too close.

These fish seem almost territorial in nature. Several times I have picked up a big chinook along one of these rocky cliffs and then caught nothing more. However, if I return to the same spot a few days later, another big one is often there. Perhaps a new "king of the rock pile" moves in to replace the one caught.

75 THE PERILS OF WEED

Many "hot" fishing areas seem to be the same areas in which a great deal of weed and debris collects. This is especially true in back eddies and tide lines, where the same forces that sweep in the plankton also bring the seaweed and other debris. Often you must troll through these areas to get to the best concentrations of fish. Downriggers are helpful in this situation because the downrigger wire will catch most of the weed and prevent it from getting to the lure itself. Another way to keep debris off your fishing line is to put the rod tip under water as you pass through areas of heavy weed. Debris is caught on the rod and can be shaken free when you get back into clean water.

Chapter Six
FISHING WITH BAIT

Detailed techniques for fishing with bait are covered quite thoroughly in my book *How to Catch Salmon: Advanced Techniques,* but I will summarize the most important secrets here.

76 | BAIT HOLDERS SCORE WELL

Top anglers can rig trolling baits with no help from a bait holder, but these plastic devices, which fit over the front end of the bait, do have a number of advantages.

For one thing, they give dependable bait action. The curve of the holder and its overall configuration give the lure a definite rolling action. (Baits used alone soften quickly and action can change dramatically so that they no longer attract fish.) Bait holders also allow a bait to be used much longer, even after bumping bottom or hitting seaweed or other debris. Natural baits alone cannot stand up to this abuse.

The most popular bait holders in B.C. are the Strip Teaser lures made by Rhys Davis of Sidney, B.C. They include the original Strip Teaser, Super Strip Teaser, Minnow Teaser, Herring Teaser, and Tiny Teaser.

Other bait holders made in B.C. include the Krippled Minnow and Krippled Anchovy made by Jim Gilbert

Enterprises, the Spring King lures made by Gordon Robinson of Sooke, the Nosky Killer, and others.

Many experienced anglers argue that bait holders are not necessary, usually because they personally have been so successful using cut-plug herring. Cut-plug herring is simply a piece of herring with its head cut off at an angle so that the remaining portion of the herring body rotates when pulled through the water. It can be extremely effective in many situations, but experiments using our underwater camera showed that the salmon preferred whole herring in a Herring Teaser head over cut-plug herring by almost four to one, even when the best cut-plugs from top guides were used.

In river mouths, I believe cut-plugs are sometimes better than whole baits, but I would add a trailing hook just at the tail fin to catch the short strikers.

77   BEST BAIT ACTION

Our underwater camera revealed that a fast rolling action was most appealing to both coho and chinook in almost every situation. The only exception might be large chinooks near spawning rivers, where they will only take bait that literally bumps them on the nose. We don't have underwater pictures of this phenomenon, but it would seem that a slow-moving bait is more effective in this instance.

It seems that a tight rolling action is more effective than a pinwheel action whereby the head of the bait goes in a small circle, and the tail in a much larger circle. In any rolling action

WRONG   RIGHT

of the bait, it is important that the head of the bait go in the same arc as the tail of the bait.

78 GET GASPING, PULSING ACTION

The tight rolling action just described should also have a beat, or pulsing action, like a gasping, twisting, wounded herring that is rolling over but hesitating ever so slightly after each roll, as though trying to regain its balance.

Because each piece of bait is somewhat different in its shape and consistency, setting up and getting an effective bait action is more a case of trial and error than it is when fishing with other lures. It's even difficult to show proper bait action in the two-dimensional, still-action illustrations in this book. A live demonstration in a water-filled tank or an actual fishing trip is by far the best way to learn.

I used to take all my fishing students on a field trip so we could demonstrate proper lure action and indeed the entire fishing procedure in a real-life situation. It was a wonderful experience for both students and teacher ... we all learned a great deal and inevitably had a beautiful day on the water.

When my fishing classes began to average over 200 students, it became impossible to take them all out on the boat, but I'd still love to do it if it were possible.

79 USING BAITS WITH FLASHERS AND DODGERS

As I've already mentioned, I do not use flashers or dodgers (except on my downrigger), because playing a fish is much more enjoyable without them. However, there is no question that a flasher or dodger will sometimes enhance a bait's action by giving that extra little kick when it may not otherwise be working quite right. Yet it can also dampen the action, and in some cases it will scare off salmon, especially big ones: Our camera showed that they tended to shy away.

If you do use flashers or dodgers, it is extremely important to get the bait working well on its own. You can do this by holding a flasher in your hand and putting it in the water with the edge knifing parallel to the water. This will allow the bait to roll normally without the added action of the flasher. You can then make adjustments as necessary before fishing it with the flasher or dodger.

80 TAKE CARE OF BAITS

Herring and anchovy baits are getting extremely expensive, sometimes costing two to three dollars for a package of a half-dozen. Herring baits should be kept in a small, insulated bait box with an artificial ice pack on top. Thaw only a few pieces of bait at a time, keeping the rest frozen. This is especially important when using whole herring or anchovy baits, since they soften much faster than strip baits.

Any bait not used can be refrozen. I often refreeze even the herring strips that have already thawed and have actually been used in the water, providing they are still in good shape. I have sometimes refrozen the same bait two or three times without apparent harm to its fish-catching ability.

Another effective method of keeping bait for future use is salting it. After returning from fishing, place thawed strips or whole baits on a bed of coarse salt and then cover them with another layer of salt. This preserves the baits and also tends to toughen them a bit. Keep them in the refrigerator or a cool place, and they will last at least a week. This method seems especially effective with whole baits, somewhat counteracting their tendency to go soft and mushy.

81 ADJUST BAIT ACTION

Watching the lure roll beside the boat is important in any trolling situation, but it is absolutely vital each time you put out a piece of natural bait. More often than not, I make some adjustment to the bait or bait holder before putting it down each time. Lure action can be modified in the following ways.

✧ Change hook position. Moving the hook toward the tail of the bait will slow down the rolling action; pulling it forward will speed up the roll. This changes the weight balance of the lure as a whole.

✧ Change the shape of the bait holder. Plastic bait holders can be twisted by hand to give them more or less bend. (Increasing the bend will speed up the roll.) You can also make more permanent adjustments to bait holders by steaming them over a kettle to get the desired modification. You might even prepare a template to modify all your bait holders if you find a real "killer" action.

✧ Modify the bait. Sometimes you can cut just a quarter- or half-inch off the head or the tail of a piece of herring strip to speed up its action. I sometimes trim the tail and cut the meat very thin to improve the action.

With whole herring or anchovy bait, you can sometimes alter the action by jamming it tighter into the bait holder, which causes a slight weight transfer. You can also adjust the bend in whole bait by tightening or loosening the hook on which it's impaled.

Whole-bait action also changes dramatically depending on where the hook is placed in the minnow. The hook can also be inserted into herring strip, but this does hamper some of the natural wiggling action that makes a strip bait so appealing.

Using a larger or heavier hook will slow bait action, while a lighter, smaller hook will speed it up. Adding a trailer hook behind the main one will slow down bait action.

The easiest of these adjustments is the first—moving the position of the hook. It's the method I used to use most of the time. Here again, however, my underwater camera has changed my fishing technique. Because most salmon attack a bait from the tail, I want to get my hook as close to the tail as possible. Finicky feeders also tend to nip lightly at the last quarter-inch of the bait and simply let go unless a hook is right there. This is usually what is happening when you see your rod tip dip back momentarily as though you had a nibble. Many experts once claimed dogmatically that this rod-tip action was indicative of a salmon slapping the bait with its tail before striking—until the underwater camera showed otherwise.

Now I adjust my baits by bending the plastic head or cutting the strip itself, or I even change the action by adjusting boat speed. I do want to keep that hook right at the tail of the bait, and keep it sticky-sharp.

Chapter Seven
MATURE SALMON IN RIVER-MOUTH AREAS

When salmon approach their home rivers and streams, dramatic changes occur, both physically and in their behaviour patterns. Initially, the salmon begin to darken in colour, especially toward the belly. The upper jaw begins to hook over, and sometimes both jaws change shape, making the fish into a rather fierce-looking beast. Eventually, as they move upstream to the spawning grounds, the flesh begins to deteriorate.

The change most important to an angler relates to the salmon's apparent lack of interest in feeding. While they will still strike at lures or baits in certain circumstances, almost

NOT TODAY -- I HAVE A ... ER... A HEADACHE!

all fish caught in river-mouth areas have empty stomachs. Obviously, their feeding instinct has been turned off and they are striking for other reasons. Of course, their major drive is to get to the spawning grounds to lay eggs and deposit milt, in nature's wondrous miracle of the renewal of life. (If reproduction is a once-in-a-lifetime occurrence for salmon, no wonder its attention is focused on it ... tonight's the night!)

82 TROLL SLOWLY FOR RIVER-MOUTH CHINOOKS

Big mature chinooks lying in holding pools near river mouths (or even in the last few miles before arriving at the river) will not chase a bait like actively feeding fish will. However, their instinct and lifetime of voracious feeding might trigger them to strike if we make the bait especially hard to resist.

We do this by presenting the fish with a lazy, rolling bait or lure that moves slowly through the water. Hopefully, we will be able to troll it close enough to the big chinook that taking the lure requires no special effort on its part. This is why it is so important to be in exactly the right spot when fishing for mature chinook. If you don't take the lure literally right past its nose, you won't get any action. Usually these holding spots are well known to local fishermen, and many boats (sometimes hundreds) jockey for position over the hot spot. This is why mooching and driftfishing or jigging are often productive in estuaries, as anglers try to sit right over the hot spot, keeping their lures working in the holding pool rather than trolling in and out of it.

83 FISH AGAINST THE BANK

Pre-spawning chinook usually migrate tight against the shoreline, even many miles from their spawning river. Studies show that salmon fingerlings migrate close to the bank on their way downstream, and spawning adults apparently use the same route on the way back. They are sometimes in quite shallow water. I remember hooking one 40-pound chinook while trolling in a small aluminum boat under some overhanging trees. In fact, my rod hit a tree limb as I snapped it back to set the hook.

When fish gather at a river mouth, they usually lie in a deep pool just at the edge of alluvial silt deposits from the river. As the fresh water mixes with the salt and spreads out into a bay, the water velocity slows and the mud and silt from the river drop to the bottom, forming a shelf against which the salmon lie.

Fishing regulations often prohibit fishing right at the river mouth itself. This is justified, in my opinion, since these big spawners are vulnerable to snagging and other harassment in this confined area. However, if regulations permit, you can sometimes anchor your boat at the top of the silt shelf and drift right over the holding pool.

84 | LEAVE THE CROWDS BEHIND

If a favourite holding area for big chinooks is crowded with boats that have been working it incessantly for several hours, you might try moving a few hundred feet away from the congested area. I think that big salmon lying in such a pool will sometimes move a short distance away to escape the plethora of lures trolling back and forth through their resting spot. The vibration from all the motors may also make them uncomfortable enough to move. But after they have settled into their new spot, there is always the chance that your lure will tempt them.

85 | BE FIRST ON THE WATER

As already mentioned, the first two hours after daybreak are often the most productive for catching fish. This is especially true in estuaries. Migrating fish often move during the night, and a fresh run of fish could be there waiting for the early-bird angler. The fish will have burned up a lot of energy getting to the holding pool and are more likely to strike than those that have already settled in. The first lures through the pool in the morning have an excellent chance of tempting these fish to strike.

New fish may move into the holding pool at any time of the day, so it's worth coming back again after a few hours, especially if early-morning pressure has been heavy and the boats have moved to other areas after the morning bite is over. You can sometimes pick up a fish that has moved in during the lull.

Fishing during tide changes and in late evening can also be productive for the simple reason that the pre-spawning salmon do not shed their lifetime instincts completely and thus might be tempted by a lure at these traditional feeding times.

86 | NATURAL BAITS ARE BEST

All fishing techniques are based on a certain amount of deception, of tricking the fish into believing that your lure is its natural food. If you are trolling slowly, the fish has maximum opportunity to look over your lure. Its natural wariness and a lifetime of successfully avoiding lures make the wily salmon a pretty tough customer to fool.

While some artificial lures are often productive in river-mouth areas, natural bait attracts the most fish by far, mainly because it's closest to the real thing. A natural bait trolled inches from a salmon's nose is probably the most difficult for it to resist.

Many anglers use cut-plug herring and mooch it slowly back and forth across the holding pools. Often they cut their baits right on the fishing grounds and discard the herring heads over the side. On at least three occasions I have cleaned large salmon and found these discarded herring heads in their stomachs. One 35-pounder had seven herring heads in its stomach and had probably been sitting down there gulping up the tasty morsels as they drifted past his mouth. Then my rolling Herring Teaser came by, and the fish made its big mistake.

87 | PERSISTENCE PAYS OFF

The most popular theory holds that pre-spawners strike because they are irritated by the lure and strike out in anger. I don't think this is their primary motivation, but I *do* think they strike at lures for reasons other than feeding.

I recall one beautiful morning on Englishman River near Parksville on Vancouver Island. I was casting for steelhead trout in a crystal-clear pool, gunning in particular for a large steelhead lying at the edge of a riffle. I made at least 100 casts near the fish, with the Daredevle lure sometimes passing within a foot of its nose. The steelhead ignored it completely. After casting to several other areas of the pool, I returned for one last crack at the big steelhead. As the lure fluttered past the fish, it suddenly turned and snapped at the lure with a motion that indicated pure anger or frustration. I was so startled, I almost let the fish jerk the rod from my hand before recovering to enjoy an adrenalin-pumping battle that only a fresh-run river steelhead can muster.

When crowds of boats continually troll or jig in a confined holding pool, the lures must be almost bumping into the fish time and time again. It seems hard to believe that they wouldn't strike out in frustration at least once in a while.

There is another theory that pre-spawning salmon will strike out as a protective reaction. We know, for instance, that cutthroat trout move upriver behind the salmon, often stealing their eggs on the spawning grounds. They have even been known to bump the ripe females in an attempt to dislodge their eggs. This is another reason why large, herring-like baits are effective in estuary areas. A salmon might think the bait is a cutthroat trout and strike out in an instinctive reaction to protect its eggs.

I sometimes think it's a shame to harass the salmon in this manner, but there is no question that dogged persistence may sometimes trigger a strike out of frustration or protective instinct.

88 | FISH FAST FOR HOOK-NOSED COHO

River-mouth coho can often be taken using the same tactics described for pre-spawning chinook. In fact, the coho that set a world record was a 31-pounder taken in this manner in Cowichan Bay on Vancouver Island. Patty Hallberg (wife of Lee Hallberg, the "Old Fisherman" radio commentator) had given up trolling bucktails for coho and decided to go deep and slow-troll for big chinook when her record-setting fish struck.

However, successful coho anglers often troll at breakneck speeds with bucktail flies and abalone spinners for big, hooknosed coho in estuary areas. Trolling Flatfish (U-20 size, orange with black spots, is a real killer) or other shovel-nosed lures at accelerated speeds can also bring successful results.

Even drift fishermen who usually get their strikes as their lures flutter to the bottom have found that they can take coho by casting out and retrieving just as fast as they can crank their big, heavy-duty saltwater spinning reels.

Chapter Eight
STRIKING, PLAYING, AND LANDING A FISH

If you have been studying and putting into practice the tips described thus far, you should already be experiencing one of the greatest thrills in fishing: the actual moment of strike. But after going through all of the preparation and development of proper lure techniques, you don't want to miss the big payoff.

89 | SETTING THE HOOK

Salmon will take a lure in a number of different ways, and it is important for the angler to set the hook properly in each instance.

Our underwater studies show that more than 80 percent of salmon attack from the rear, sometimes just nipping at the tail and sometimes completely engulfing the entire lure. As soon as its mouth touches the metal hook, the fish reacts in what looks like pure panic. Its gills fly out, its mouth snaps open, and the salmon shakes its head vigorously to get rid of the foreign substance. (It's been eating herring and baitfish all its life, and this is the first one that has nipped back. No wonder it's frightened.)

A sticky-sharp hook is the most important thing you can have in preparation for this moment. A hook that isn't sharp enough to "stick" will merely skid out of the salmon's mouth. Once the hook sticks, the fish's thrashing will help make the hook penetrate deeper. If you are fishing with a downrigger and a firmly attached release clip, the hook will often set

POINT OF BRAND-NEW HOOK

POINT OF A STICKY-SHARP HOOK

itself from the force of the fish tripping the release pin. The same is true if you are trolling with heavy weights or are trolling at a fast speed. The heavy weight or fast-moving boat will provide enough resistance to embed the hook.

However, slower trolling, light-tackle trolling, or low-friction downrigger releases need help from the angler to get a solid hookup. In my opinion, it is best to set the hook on any strike. This ensures that the fish is properly hooked before the exciting battle begins.

If you are fishing with a downrigger or using another technique where there might be some slack in the line, reel in as fast as you can until the line is tight, point the rod at the fish, and set the hook by a series of sharp, short, upward tugs, ending with the rod butt pointing back over your shoulder and the tip bowed straight toward the fish. This series of jerks will progressively pull the hook past the barb and make it far more difficult for the fish to throw the hook on any subsequent slack line.

If you are fishing live bait that has small hooks embedded into a swimming baitfish, the salmon will often grab it tentatively and hold it in its jaw for a moment before turning it to swallow the bait headfirst. In this situation it is important to strip a bit of slack line so the fish feels no resistance. Then, when the line begins to move off steadily, set the hook hard.

The same is true with certain slow-trolling techniques using frozen baits or cut-plug herring. If the hooks are well buried in the bait, it is probably best to allow the fish to ingest it fully before driving the hook home.

My own preference, however, when using Strip Teaser plastic heads in front of a trolled lure, is to set the hook immediately upon feeling the strike. With my sticky-sharp trailing hooks, the fish usually has the point inside its mouth on the first touch, and I want to set the hook before it's spit out.

In downrigger fishing, you can't react fast enough to set the hook because the line must first be released from the downrigger to get a direct pull on the fish. In this case, you must wait until the fish is hooked at least enough to pull on the release pin, then finish the job as just described.

90 | KEEP YOUR ROD UP

This piece of advice has been given in almost every fishing book ever written. It is, however, the single most important factor in successfully playing any game fish.

The fishing rod is like a giant rubber band or shock absorber. Holding the butt vertical allows the rod to bend through a full 90-degree arc, absorbing the sudden runs and lunges of the fish without breaking the line or allowing it to go slack. It gives the angler that extra split second to wind in or let out line and maintain an even pressure on the fish.

Lowering the rod toward the fish removes this shock-absorber effect and allows no margin of error in handling the reel. Yet it is amazing how many anglers let the rod drop in reaction to a hard run of the fish or as their arms tire after a

"SHOCK ABSORBER"
EFFECT OF
ROD FLEXING
PROTECTS
LINE

NO FLEXIBILITY.--
LINE ALONE MUST
TRY TO ABSORB
PULL OF FISH

lengthy fight. I have watched far too many big fish snap the line with a sudden lunge as a tiring angler lowers his rod when the fish nears the boat.

91 LIGHTLY DOES IT

My favourite reels are the single-action type, which allow me to feel every movement of the fish and provide complete control of the tension at all times. This is one of the great excitements of fishing, feeling the reel spinning as I palm it and apply a gentle braking action.

I hold the rod above the reel and keep the butt against my hip or abdomen to give me some leverage. As the fish starts to run, I feel it instantly with the hand holding the rod and get my fingers off the reel handles to begin the palming action. As my rod hand feels the line tension easing, I reverse the procedure and begin winding in. All of this action becomes automatic with a little practise, and the reel hand moves smoothly between reel handles and edge of the spool (for palming). It's almost like playing a musical instrument ... and the music is very sweet.

I have used several popular brands of single-action reel, and they performed satisfactorily except that the friction drags were undependable. I used my hand as the primary brake, but it was disconcerting to have the drag setting on the reel keep changing itself.

This came to an end when I was presented with, as a gift, a new Islander reel made here on Vancouver Island. I could not believe the difference a smooth drag can make in handling a fighting fish on light tackle. Now that I am getting close to 77 years of age, I'm relearning an old truth: Quality tackle is well worth the price!

If you are using a star-drag or spinning reel with a slipping clutch, the drag should be set before starting to fish and left alone during the action. A good way to test the drag setting is to pull line off the reel and watch the rod tip. If the tip remains relatively stable, the drag is smooth, but if it jerks up and down, it is obviously sticking and is probably set too tight.

With a flexible rod tip the drag should be set at only two or three pounds of tension, and perhaps even less if you want to really enjoy playing the fish. I built a special device for testing the amount of bend in a rod at various line tensions. We were amazed to find that an eight- or nine-foot rod with a firm butt and limber tip will be bent double at a pressure well under five pounds.

Setting a light drag on the reel allows you to have at least some of the fun of a single-action reel by using your thumb on the spool to apply additional pressure when controlling the fish.

One of the biggest mistakes made with star-drag reels is to tighten the drag when a stubborn fish refuses to come toward the boat. The over-tightened drag gives much more control of the fish, but a sudden lunge near the boat will often snap the line before the angler can readjust the drag setting. For this reason, it's far better to use a light drag and your thumb for additional pressure, which can be released instantly in such circumstances.

I fish for fun and do everything I can to increase my enjoyment when playing a fish. To me, a single-action reel provides that extra thrill, and I highly recommend that everyone at least give it a try.

92 PRACTISE FIRST

As a charter guide, I often worked extremely hard to find the fish and get a good salmon hooked and on the line. Just as I was feeling satisfied with myself, the angler would jam his hand into the reel handles to stop a hard-running fish, and it would be gone (usually with one of my favourite lures)!

An exhilarating moment of success was thus turned into an embarrassing failure for the angler, who often turned his wrath on me, blaming a weak line, poor knot, or improperly oiled reel. I listened to these complaints with a weak smile, knowing that all of these factors had been checked thoroughly beforehand.

Then I adopted a practice that drastically reduced the incidence of lost fish. I asked each neophyte angler to practise playing the fish right on the dock before we headed for the fishing grounds. I would ask him to hold the rod up while I pulled the line and raced up and down the dock like a maniac. They learned proper fish-playing techniques. Surprisingly, it took only a minute or two for most people to get the hang of it.

A few years ago, I developed a device to train fishermen to play fish, and it has become a popular game for bars, sporting-goods stores, and outdoor shows. It's called the Sport Fish Simulator, and there are more than 300 of them in use around the world, from New Zealand to Finland. A TV screen shows an underwater picture of a fish approaching and striking a bait or lure. The angler stands in front of the screen, holding a rod and reel with the line going to a box under the TV. As the fish strikes, the line runs out and the angler "plays" the fish on the screen. The machine scores the angler's skill. The Simulator has become a major training device as well as a popular game.

93 | LET HIM RUN

When I was a fishing guide, I got just as excited as my customers did when a fish struck and was on the line. I would excitedly and continuously shout two pieces of advice. One was "keep your rod up" and the other was "let him run." This is the moment we have been waiting for. We want to enjoy every moment and let the fish run and play, allowing us to feel the surging rod and screaming reel.

Many anglers take fishing so seriously that they can't enjoy their fish. They grind furiously, forcing the fish toward the boat as fast as they can. They somehow feel that getting maximum poundage in the boat as quickly as possible is the purpose of fishing. Realists in the sport-fishing fraternity realize that the actual cost of sport-caught salmon is probably *more than $50 a pound,* so if meat is the object, buy it at the fish market and take up sailing or golf.

Letting the fish run is also sensible from a practical point of view. A fish is easier to handle on a longer line, and the stretch of the nylon gives an additional shock-absorbing effect. Forcing a fish in quickly leaves you with a wild bucking bronco on a very short line right next to the boat. There is little margin for error in line stretch or even rod action. The fish can also dash frantically under the boat or into the propellers. It is far better to have the salmon tired and docile from lots of running away from the boat.

If you are fishing in a crowd of boats, a long line can be troublesome because other craft can troll right over it and cut off the fish. In this situation, it is wise to keep the motor in gear and follow the fish out and away from the crowd.

94 | KEEP THE FISH MOVING

Sometimes a salmon will make a good run, then simply "dog it" and just lie out there shaking its head or pulling slowly and firmly against the line. Big fish will often "sound" to the bottom and then doggedly tug away. We have underwater pictures of fish swimming directly opposite to the direction of the line, maintaining just enough pressure to hold their position but not moving anywhere. In this situation I like to keep the fish moving. Gills are a most inefficient breathing apparatus, and they slam shut when the fish swims rapidly. If you can keep the fish moving, it will expend its energy in a more spectacular and enjoyable fight and come to the boat well played out.

Often, a large chinook will head straight for the bottom, leaving you directly above pulling straight up while the fish tries to bury its nose in the bottom. You can use several tactics to get the fish moving again.

✦ Thump on the butt of the rod with the flat of your palm, transmitting a shock wave through the rod and line to the fish.

✧ Strum the line by grabbing it just above the reel, pulling it sideways a foot or two, then letting go suddenly with a snap, which is transmitted to the fish.

✧ Move the boat off to the side. This tactic, probably the most effective, allows you to pull at a side angle on the fish, diverting it from its bottom-rubbing manoeuvre by forcing its head to one side. Usually the fish will take off in a driving run, sometimes heading straight for the surface.

95 PLAY THE FISH TO THE STERN

Using small boats (under about fourteen feet in length), it doesn't matter in which direction the fish is running. You can swing the rod in any direction to clear the bow or stern as needed. However, larger boats with cabins or canvas and plastic rain covers can be a major problem if the fish runs toward the bow. You may have to put the boat in gear and turn it so that the angler is always facing the fish off the stern of the boat.

If the fish runs under the boat or starts heading across the bow, plunge the rod tip down deep in the water so that the line will clear the hull and propellers. You can then work the line around the stern (with the rod tip straight down) and move to the opposite side of the boat to play the fish in the clear again.

There is one important exception to the rule to keep the rod up. When a fish jumps close to the boat, the entire line can pop free of the water's surface and run straight from the rod tip to the fish with no line friction from the water. The rod tip will usually spring back straight, and the natural tendency for the angler is to pull back farther to maintain a bend in the rod. This leaves a short taut line that can break or tear out the hooks as the fish drops back into the water. The obvious solution is to drop the rod tip quickly when the fish jumps and allow a momentary slack line, recovering tension immediately as the fish enters the water.

96 | STEADY ON THE NET

Many salmon, especially large ones, are lost at the boat when excited anglers try to net them too soon. Thrusting a net at a lively fish usually results in disaster. The fish immediately panics at the sight and sound of the net hitting the water and moving toward it. With one sweep of its powerful tail, the fish can rush off with surprising force and speed, sometimes rushing right past a portion of the net where trailing hooks might catch in the mesh ... and the fish is gone.

The angler on the rod instinctively tries to hold back the rushing fish for the netter, often resulting in broken line or torn-out hooks. When bringing a fish to net, I don't usually have my hands on the reel at all, using them instead to guide the rod and the fish toward the net. If the fish runs, the reel is free to spin out.

97 | NET THE FISH HEADFIRST

Smaller salmon under about three pounds can often be netted just by scooping the net under the fish's body. Larger fish, however, should *always* be netted headfirst. Moreover, the fish should be tired enough that it's lying on its side or back and is relatively easy to control.

98 | DO NOT LIFT THE FISH'S HEAD

Do not lift the fish's head out of the water, as this puts additional strain on the rod and can also cause the fish to thrash suddenly when it discovers its gills are clear of the water and it can no longer breathe. Just put enough tension on the rod to keep the salmon's head at the surface, then lead it gently toward the net.

The net should be slid quietly but quickly into the water at about a 45-degree angle. When half of the fish's body is over the rim of the net, you can slack off the rod tension and the fish will swim right into the bag of the net.

If you attempt to net a fish tail first (even a completely exhausted specimen), it will most likely make one last sweep of its tail when it hits the net mesh. The fish's tail thrusting against the mesh acts just like a diving board and will catapult the fish right out of the net. If some extra hooks happen to be near the mesh, they can hang up and tear loose from the fish.

99 | DON'T PUT A STRAIN ON THE NET HANDLE

After the fish is in the net, do not lift it like a shovel full of dirt. This puts a tremendous strain on the handle and could likely bend it or even break it off.

It is much better to lift the net vertically so the fish is trapped in the bag. Then reach down and grab the rim of the net to lift the fish aboard.

If you want to be *classy*, hit the fish over the head before lifting it into the boat. This prevents it from thrashing around in the net and knocking off scales, and you are left with a beautiful fish to show off.

100 | KILL IT CLEANLY

Salmon should be dispatched with a sharp blow right between the eyes. Many fishermen hit the fish too far back on the head, which will not necessarily kill it and may leave the angler bashing repeatedly at the twisting, flopping fish. A misplaced blow will also cause a blood bruise in the prime flesh just back of the head.

101 | RELEASE SMALL FISH GENTLY

If you hook an undersized fish, it will have a far better chance of surviving if it is not touched by your hands or even the landing net.

Grasp the line near the hook and lift the fish out of the water. Then use a small gaff hook or special hook releaser (see illustration) that is slid down the line to the hook and twisted upward so the fish falls free. Many anglers believe that if the fish swims away after release, it has survived. My experience while operating the Undersea Gardens proved otherwise.

We often went on fishing expeditions to capture live salmon as specimens for our exhibits. We hooked and landed them with extreme care, placing them live in a large tank with circulating, oxygenated water. We would put them into the display area in apparently excellent health. But within three or four days some of them would begin to develop fungus growth, sometimes in the shape of individual fingerprints where they had been held too tightly. Others would show fungus marks corresponding to net abrasion. Within a week or ten days, the fungus would spread into the gill cavity and the fish would die.

I often feel that fishing regulations are unrealistic in requiring anglers to release injured salmon that have no possibility of surviving, since even those that are handled carefully are quite vulnerable to disease if the protective slime on their skin is disturbed. However, fisheries officers claim—and quite justifiably—that if wounded fish were excepted from the rules, any angler could deliberately injure undersized fish and be within the law in keeping them.

Perhaps the rules should be changed to give fishermen some option in keeping wounded fish and counting them toward his daily limit. It's not a perfect answer, but it seems better than feeding the dogfish and seals.

102 CARING FOR YOUR FISH

Bringing meat home for the frying pan is not the prime goal of most recreational anglers, but enjoying the harvest of a good day's fishing is certainly one of the great joys of the sport. Fresh salmon is an exquisite delicacy, prized by gourmet chefs all over the world. They would be absolutely shocked to see the way many anglers treat their catch. Following are some important *do's* and *don'ts* for taking care of the catch.

✧ Don't drop the fish on the deck or throw it into a fish box. This will bruise the flesh and soften the meat. This rough handling is one of the reasons why seine-caught commercial fish are worth less than tenderly handled commercial troll fish.

✧ Bleed your fish. Immediately after dispatching the fish, it is a good idea to tear a gill raker loose or slit the fish's throat. This lets it bleed and improves the quality and flavour of the meat. It can be a messy practice, but many anglers believe it is well worth the trouble it takes.

✧ Wipe the slime from the fish. In the rough-and-tumble action of a day's fishing, few anglers bother to wipe down their fish on the fishing grounds, but it should certainly be done during a lull in action or upon returning to the dock.

✧ Do not store freshly caught fish in plastic bags. The chemical changes that take place in a fish's body immediately after it's caught need air circulation, especially before the fish has been cleaned. Fish stored in plastic bags goes soft very quickly.

✧ Never leave fish in the sun. Fish should be stored in an insulated fish box if possible, with ice or artificial ice packs on top. A wet cloth or burlap bag will serve a similar purpose as evaporation cools the fish. The cloth should be moistened regularly. By all means, keep the fish box in a shaded area if at all possible. If you're fishing in an open boat, you can often cover the fish box with your coat if the weather warms up. You don't need the coat yourself, and it will provide the fish with some protection against the sun and heat.

✧ Keep fish off the bottom of the fish box by using a raised platform. I sometimes use aluminum refrigerator shelving for this purpose. However, any wood, metal, or plastic frame can be used to hold the fish above the water, blood, and slime that gathers in the bottom of a fish box. The bacteria count rises quickly in such fluid, causing the flesh to deteriorate and soften.

If you are using crushed ice (as opposed to artificial plastic pouches), you will need a larger area under the platform to collect the melting ice water.

103 | CLEAN FISH IMMEDIATELY

Immediately after returning to shore, gut the fish, clean off the slime, and pat the fish dry before storing it in plastic bags or newspaper. As soon as you get home, cut up the fish and put it in the refrigerator, or store it in plastic bags in the freezer, being sure to squeeze all the air out of the bags before freezing.

Some anglers put a water glaze on their fish, especially if they have a trophy salmon they wish to serve on a special occasion at a later date. Fish can be glazed by sharp-freezing the carcass, then spraying it with a fine mist and refreezing. Repeat this procedure several times, until a thin glaze of ice builds up around the fish. This keeps it in prime shape for many months.

Chapter Nine
CONCLUSIONS

We are still working with our underwater camera to learn even more about fish behaviour. Two of our feature-length films, *Why Fish Strike! ... Why They Don't* and *In Search of the Ultimate Lure,* are now available on video. As the fish actually take the lure, close up and in slow motion, they demonstrate many of the secrets I have described.

In our research we discovered four basic strike triggers, which seem to motivate not only salmon to attack a bait, but all predatory game fish in both fresh and salt water.

The right shape of lure: Fish attack the lure that most closely resembles the shape of the baitfish on which they are feeding. Our The Lure trolling model is cast from an actual herring, and we found it most effective in areas where herring were present. Similarly, lures shaped like needlefish (candlefish, sand lance) were most effective over sandy-bottom areas where needlefish are plentiful.

A wounded-fish action: When a herring, anchovy, needlefish, or other baitfish is wounded, it loses its equilibrium. Just as a drunken person becomes wobbly on his feet, a wounded baitfish has difficulty remaining upright. As it falls over on its side, it often gives a thrust with its tail. This action can result in the fish darting off in any direction, but it often starts the fish in a rolling, spinning motion almost like a drill bit moving through the water. This characteristic motion signals the predatory game fish that its potential prey is wounded and will be relatively easy to catch.

Sonic vibration: The rapid beating, drumming action of a small spinner puts out a vibration in the water that attracts predators from a long distance away. I believe this vibration simulates the tail beats of a frightened baitfish.

While we can see for miles on land, underwater visibility is quite limited, usually 25 feet or less in the North Pacific. Even in extremely clear conditions, it seldom exceeds 100 feet. Sound, by contrast, travels farther and faster in water than in air. Sound waves from a spinner (or a flasher) can travel up to 1,000 feet or more through the denser medium of water.

I believe that the final strike decision is made by sight as the fish studies the bait, but a sonic vibration will attract fish from well beyond the sight range.

A lure with a forked tail: One or more of the three strike triggers just described are known and have been used by many fishing experts, but this last strike trigger is, we believe, unique to our research.

We studied various parts of a baitfish anatomy to determine if any particular feature was more important in triggering strikes. We put huge eyes on some baits, bright reflective artificial scales on others, and exaggerated tail fins on still others.

The only body feature that made any difference was the tail. A wiggling tail seemed to attract fish. When we put a forked notch in our artificial tail fins, fish preferred it to other shapes.

We studied as many of the popular salmon lures as we could but could not find any that utilized all four of these strike triggers. As a result, we designed our own prototypes of a radically different lure that combined as much as possible the strike triggers we had discovered. We called it The Lure. It has the exact shape of a herring, is curved to give a wounded fish roll, and has a forked-tail spinner at the back.

It has proved successful in some circumstances, and not so successful in others. Charter-boat operators on Lake Ontario found it was often extremely productive at trolling speeds of between 1.7 and 2.2 knots. Some of the top guides in Campbell River, B.C., who normally use live herring or cut-plug herring, have found The Lure extremely effective when the water is somewhat cloudy or when there is a chop. In these circumstances, The Lure can produce limit catches while normally deadly natural baits catch nothing.

While most of our lure tests were done in salt water, we are getting success stories from freshwater anglers across Canada and the northern United States. They report that our lure is often very productive on large lake trout, rainbow trout, northern pike, and even black bass.

Many of these freshwater anglers are used to casting rather than trolling, and some have had problems with line twists when they do not put a swivel up the line from this rolling-action lure.

Scent: There is no doubt in my mind that scent is important in attracting strikes. Tests with our underwater camera showed that it is difficult to repel fish with supposedly bad odours such as oil and gas, but that fish can be attracted with various compounds of amino acids.

I lectured for more than ten years at the School of Fisheries at University of Washington and showed its biologists some of my underwater tests with scent. They agreed with my conclusions and told me of their own experiments.

They believe that scent is one of the primary means of stimulating fish to feed. They developed, under a grant from the fish farmers, a formula that, when fed to farmed salmon, increased their feeding by as much as 40 percent. I obtained access to their formula and put it into Formula X-10, a scent attractant for salmon, halibut, trout, and other game fish. Berkeley has also developed a line of scent products called Strike.

Jigging Lures

Our camera is designed on the principle of an airplane wing and works best when trolling. We use planing fins, buoyancy tanks, weights, and rudders to control the direction of the camera and keep it aimed at the lures.

However, jigging, or driftfishing, is becoming extremely popular, and we wanted to study fish striking these lures. Jigging is simply lifting and dropping a lure from an anchored or slowly drifting boat, and our camera could not be controlled under these conditions. After much difficulty and experimentation, we were able to rig the camera to give us some pictures of salmon striking jigging lures. We were surprised to discover that the fish had difficulty *catching* the lures. These lead jigs dart quickly and erratically, and the fish were often unable to change direction quickly enough to intercept them.

We also found that the fish would chase them vigorously for a minute or two and then completely ignore them. If, however, we put down a fresh lure after they stopped chasing our first lure, they would begin actively chasing the new one. Based on this information, I would change lures every five minutes or so or move to a new location rather than continually jigging the same lure in the same location.

As a result of this limited research, we worked at designing a jigging lure that would overcome this fast darting problem. We tried lures made from lighter-weight material, but they were difficult to keep in position, prone to being swept away by the tide or current.

We finally hit upon the idea of using a spinner similar to the one on our trolling lure. This forked-tail spinner solved many of the problems of conventional jigging lures. The

Needlefish

Anchovy/Herring

spinner slowed down and controlled the darting action and gave the fish a steadier target at the tail of the lure where the sharp hooks are waiting. The spinner also provided a sonic attracter, and its forked tail was a visual trigger. I have been using this new design and find it very effective.

Chapter 10
FUTURE PLANS

In earlier editions of this book, this chapter was filled with many exciting plans, many of which have been carried out. We went to South Australia to film the great white shark with world-famous shark hunter Rodney Fox and got material for an exciting new documentary, *Why Sharks Attack, Why They Don't!*

The big man-eating sharks were far more cautious than we had expected, but we did get some dramatic footage and learned that sharks are attracted by some of the same stimulants that trigger salmon to strike. They were attracted to erratic, wounded-fish movements and to scents—but they would not strike the source of a scent unless it was shaped like a fish. Vibration also triggered them to attack.

We have done more underwater camera research, but my work has led to seven companies making underwater cameras for fishermen, so the field is getting saturated. As I approach my 78th birthday I'm slowing down a bit, but still doing tests on prawn feeding and fish migration.

I'm also continuing my seminars in the Northwest, doing presentations for Boeing and for local schools. I do an annual *Living off the Sea!* series of seminars in my home town of Sidney, some in my own living room, and some in the new Charlie White Theatre in Sidney.

I've got a new 28-foot Bayliner trophy with four (count 'em, four!) outboards. Two are used to get to the fishing grounds at 30 knots, and the other two, on each side of the transom, are for trolling and for keeping the boat straight in a crosswind. I guess these are my "retirement" years, and I'm still having as much fun as ever while continuing to learn more about my beloved outdoors and the sea!

If you have questions, I may be able to answer them if you e-mail me at charliesaltaire@aol.com.

Tight lines and good fishing!

OBTAINING CURRENT FISHING REGULATIONS

Do not go fishing along the west coast without checking current government regulations.

The *B.C. Tidal Waters Sport Fishing Guide*, published annually by Fisheries and Oceans Canada, is available free of charge at sporting-goods stores, marinas, and similar outlets. The guide contains all current regulations governing sport fishing for salmon, halibut, rockfish, crabs, oysters, and other species. Check carefully the sections on spot closures, which were introduced as a conservation measure. In addition, remember that size limits apply to all salmon.

Current sport-fishing regulations are also available by visiting the following websites.

B.C. Ministry of Water, Land and Air: Fresh Water Regulations Protection
    http://www.bcfisheries.gov.bc.ca/rec/fresh/regulations/synopsis.html

Fisheries and Oceans Canada: Salt Water Regulations
    http://www-comm.pac.dfo-mpo.gc.ca/pages/sfg/default_e.htm

Alaska Department of Fish and Game
    http://www.sf.adfg.state.ak.us/statewide/html/reghome.stm

Washington Department of Fish and Wildlife
    http://www.wa.gov/wdfw/fish/regs/fishregs.htm

Oregon Department of Fish and Wildlife
    http://www.dfw.state.or.us/

California Fish and Game Commission
    http://www.dfg.ca.gov/fg_comm/fishregs.html

CHARLIE WHITE'S FISHING LOG

Date	Time	Lure and Colour	Depth	Weather & Tide

Species	Weight	Where	Remarks

THE CHARLIE WHITE LIBRARY

These books should be basic reading for any fisher, crabber, or shellfish lover on the west coast. Charlie has long been a fan of Nelson Dewey's illustrations, so his books abound with Nelson's amusing cartoons—perfect complements to Charlie's sound advice, good humour, and veteran's wisdom.

How to Catch Bottomfish

Now in a NEW format, this book is a must-have for families who love to fish. Bottomfish are easier to catch, and they are present year-round. Best of all, they are also an excellent table fish.
ISBN 1-894384-60-1
5 1/2" x 8 1/2" • 128 pages
Softcover • $15.95

How to Catch Crabs

The best part of crabbing is the payoff! Whether you use crab traps or the traditional low-tide shoreline hunt to bag your quota, this book will aid your cause. Includes tips for storing, cleaning, and cooking your catch.
ISBN 1-895811-51-1
5½" x 8½" • 64 pages
Softcover • $8.95

Visit the Heritage House website at
www.heritagehouse.ca for on-line catalogue.
Heritage books may be ordered through
bookstores across North America.

How to Catch Salmon
Advanced Techniques

The most comprehensive salmon-fishing book available! It covers everything from choosing the right equipment, baits, and lures to how to play and net a fish. Includes a chapter by guest author Jack James of Radiant Lures.

ISBN 1-894384-64-4
5 1/2" x 8 1/2" • 192 pages
Softcover • $16.95

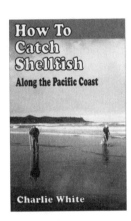

How To Catch Shellfish
Along the Pacific Coast

The Pacific coast is a gourmand's seafood playground. Disclosing his latest research, Charlie's practical guide provides all you need to know to gather a shellfish feast.

ISBN 1-895811-49-X
5 1/2" x 8 1/2" • 96 pages
Softcover • $9.95

Living Off the Sea

This popular guide includes information on how and when to harvest, accessible exotic seafoods, red tide, and even how to live off a beach if stranded. Complementing Nelson Dewey's technical illustrations are fish drawings by Chris Sherwood.

ISBN 1-895811-47-3
5 1/2" x 8 1/2" • 128 pages
Softcover • $11.95

ABOUT THE AUTHOR

Charlie White is an internationally known author, filmmaker, television personality, and fish-behaviour researcher. His books on salmon and marine life have sold more than 500,000 copies, putting him among the top authors on fishing.

Charlie also developed a series of Undersea Gardens marine exhibits in the United States and Canada, which allow viewers to descend beneath sea level to watch sea life in a natural environment.

In 1973, he began experimenting with a remote-controlled underwater television camera to study salmon strike behaviour. His underwater close-ups, in freeze frame and slow motion, revealed for the first time many fascinating new facts about how salmon and other species approach and strike various lures.

He has made three feature-length films about his work, two of which are now marketed on video (*Why Fish Strike! ... Why They Don't* and *In Search of the Ultimate Lure*). He has been recognized in *Who's Who* for his fish-behaviour studies, and he invented a number of popular fishing products, including the Scotty downrigger, Electric Hooksharp, Picture Perfect Lures, and Formula X-10 fish feeding stimulant.

The Charlie White Theatre in Sidney, B.C., which opened in 2002, honours Charlie's contribution to the community. He was also honoured by the University of Victoria as Fisherman of the Year in 2001.

Charlie lives on the waterfront near Sidney, B.C., and continues his unique underwater research on fish strike behaviour. For more information, write to Charlie c/o Heritage House, #108-17665 66A Ave., Surrey, BC, V3S 2A7, or e-mail publisher@heritagehouse.ca.